Taste Life!
Organic Recipes

VITAL HEALTH PUBLISHING
Ridgefield, CT

Taste Life! Organic Recipes

Edited by Leslie Cerier

Book Design: interior, Cathy Lombardi; cover, David Richard

Published by: Vital Health Publishing
            P.O. Box 152
            Ridgefield, CT 06877
            Website: www.vitalhealth.net
            E-mail: info@vitalhealth.net
            Phone: 203-894-1882
            Orders: 1-877-VIT-BOOK

Printed in the United States of America
ISBN: 1-890612-16-2

Table of Contents

Foreword

Food—glorious food! We all relish and enjoy the experience of eating—not only to nourish or satisfy ourselves, but also often to savor the flavors and experience the aromas. This experience can be shared—with the accompanying sights and sounds of friends, family, and even strangers—or it can be an individual pleasure—quiet and satisfying. For those of us who love to cook, all the sensual and social pleasure is heightened. For those of us who want to change the world, eating and cooking organic foods is a simple, easy and powerful choice.

And now, here is a cookbook to help you make the most of the organic ingredients that you purchase or perhaps raise in your garden. You will find you can make most any type of dish featuring organic ingredients: traditional, vegetarian, vegan, meat, wheat-free, dairy-free, and the list goes on.

As you try out these recipes using organic ingredients, you can feel proud to be a steward of the earth—protecting the environment and public health. Organic production systems replenish and maintain soil fertility, eliminate the use of toxic and persistent pesticides and fertilizers, and build biologically diverse agriculture. This means that you are helping to minimize the pollution of our air, water and natural resources from agricultural practices. The result—not only a better world in which to live today, but also a better world for those who follow.

In addition, organic food reduces your exposure to the health risks associated with pesticide residues, artificial ingredients and preservatives, antibiotics and growth hormones in meat, dairy and chicken, and chemicals used in the processing of food. Organic production systems do not allow the use of any of these materials and methods and also prohibit the use of irradiation and genetically engineered seeds and crops.

I'm convinced that the way that food is grown and prepared can change our world to one that is ecologically sound, socially just and sustainable. I purchase organic products and encourage those I know and meet to do the same. My husband, who does our grocery shopping, has been converted, and my children, grown now with children of their own, have been raised on organic products. It is a wonderful legacy to pass down to the next generation.

Food is too humble for its own good. It's such a routine part of our day that its potential to create change is, as the saying goes, hidden in plain sight. Food has extraordinary qualities as a catalyst of personal and social restoration. It has a unique power—not domination, but power that enables positive change.

Real Food for a Change by Wayne Roberts, Rod MacRae and Lori Stahlbrand.

Starting to change the world is as easy as crumbling some organic tofu or organic cheese into your salad of organic greens. There's no need or reason to delay getting started. So, try something simple, or perhaps something that tantalizes. Make a meal for your family or your friends. Throw a party for yourself, or for your neighborhood. And be prepared for something truly scrumptious—and life changing.

Enjoy!
Katherine DiMatteo

Katherine DiMatteo is executive director of the Organic Trade Association based in Greenfield, MA.

Introduction

One of the early breakthroughs in my creative life as a cook came in 1976 when I discovered an organic bakery on the upper West Side of Manhattan. This discovery led me to begin shopping in health food stores and to buying as much organic food as I could find. At first the selection was limited, but little by little an array of grains, beans, fruits, vegetables, juices, nut butters, eggs, cheeses, meats and more became commonplace. Cooking was no longer a rote exercise, but a sensual (and nourishing!) synthesis of aromas and flavors.

Over the years, more and more organic foods have found their way into supermarkets, farmers' markets, co-ops, CSAs (community supported agriculture), gourmet shops and restaurants, mail order catalogs and the Internet. It has become easy to cook everything from appetizers to desserts entirely with certified organic ingredients.

Of all my reasons for eating as much organic food as I can find, by far the most important are my vivid impressions of the beautiful scenery on organic farms. Every year, I spend as much time as I can on a sixteen-acre organic farm, the CSA that feeds my hungry family as well as 500 other households (from surrounding Western Massachusetts hill towns and the Boston area). Here, among the long rows of vegetables, beans, herbs, flowers and fruits, I can be found snacking. Basket in hand, I stroll and munch on juicy strawberries in June, sugar snap peas in July, cherry tomatoes in August, and sweet raspberries and green beans until autumn's first frost. With each weekly visit, I discover and taste something new: sweet corn; green, yellow and red peppers (hot peppers too!); cooling cucumbers; succulent watermelons; starlike borage flowers and bright orange nasturtiums; garlic chives; sugar-sweet baby carrots—the list goes on and on. But the thing that I remember most is the feeling of endless bounty and wholesomeness.

Even at home in the kitchen this happy feeling continues to emanate, and the recipes by other cooks in this book reflect it as well. Whether it is smoked salmon salad with baby potatoes, chick peas with tomatoes and ginger, or jewel-like slices of autumn vegetables in a fabulous curry-vegetable soup, the flavors express themselves precisely and clearly. Even more complicated dishes rest upon a solid foundation of organic beans and grains (whole foods), which allows their more piquant and delicate flavors to soar. Organic oils, herbs and spices add their deep, rich, lush tones. They enhance rather than overwhelm the humble vegetables.

This book also abounds in simple, healthy recipes over which there is no need to fuss—low-fat meals that require minimal preparation and clean-up time. Yet even this more basic faire offers luxurious combinations of flavors because of the high quality of its ingredients and the care with which they are combined.

Because the earth has been so generous, and organic farmers working in harmony with it have helped bring forth its goodness, little has to be done to prepare delicious meals. Anyone can do it. Simply chop, mix, stir and simmer. Then Taste Life!

Even on the raw side, from a simple green salad to the endless variations with beans, pasta, croutons and chevre, simply using organic vegetables makes the dish come alive!

Taste Life! Organic Recipes honors you, the home cook, with over 100 delicious recipes contributed by organic food enthusiasts from across the country. Using organic ingredients (grown without insecticides and fungicides), talented home cooks can easily create a healthy, tasty synergy in any dish. With their enhanced quality, organic foods deliver a full, inviting range of flavors in each bite.

The real fun begins when you turn to the recipes, start to cook—and taste the bounty of life!

Bon Santé,
Leslie

1

BREAKFAST

Peanut Butter Maple Granola
by Kemper Carlsen, Shutesbury, MA

This high-protein granola tastes like a sweet cookie. It is easy to make and is delightful for breakfast and snacks.

Vegetarian, heart smart, wheat-free, corn-free

Yields 15 cups

> 1 cup canola oil (for low fat, use 1/4 cup water and 1/2 cup oil, increase maple syrup by 1/4 cup)
> 1 cup maple syrup (if you use honey instead, use 3/4 cup)
> 1 cup peanut butter (can use other nut butters instead—even tahini)
> 1 tablespoon vanilla
> 10–12 cups rolled oats
> 1/4 teaspoon salt (use none if peanut butter is salted)
> 1 cup sunflower seeds
> 1/4 cup sesame seeds
> 2 tablespoons cinnamon, ground
> 1 tablespoon cardamom, ground

Preheat oven to 300 degrees. Combine wet ingredients and whisk until peanut butter blends in completely. Mix dry ingredients in baking pan(s) till fully combined. Add and mix in wet ingredients. (I use my hands, it's faster and easier.) Put baking pans in oven. Bake 30 to 45 minutes, stirring frequently to avoid edges getting toasted before the rest.

Blueberry Breeze
by Denise Roseland, Lakewinds Natural Foods, Minnetonka, MN

Breakfast smoothie, yum! Add optional ice cubes if you want it thick like a shake.

Vegetarian, wheat-free, corn-free

Serves 2

> 2 bananas
> 1/2 cup fresh or frozen blueberries

1/2 cup vanilla yogurt
1 1/2 cups milk, soy or rice milk
2 tablespoons wheat germ or bran
Optional: A few ice cubes

Put all the ingredients in a blender and puree till smooth.

Blueberry Chick Pea Pancakes
by David Richard, Ridgefield, CT

Made with chick pea paste or flour, these pancakes are nutritious—and delicious!

Vegetarian, wheat-free, corn-free, heart smart

Makes a dozen 3- to 4-inch pancakes

1 cup of chick pea (garbanzo bean) flour*
(You can also combine 1/2 cup chick pea flour with 1/2 cup brown rice, buckwheat or millet flours.)
3/4–1 cup rice, soy or almond milk
1 large egg
1 tablespoon expeller-pressed oil
1/2 teaspoon gluten-free baking powder
1 quart of fresh blueberries or 1 8-ounce bag of frozen blueberries, defrosted

*If you are a "from-scratch" chef, you can make a chick pea paste by soaking a cup or two of chick peas the day or night before (6–8 hours) and boiling the chick peas for a couple of hours and then mashing by hand or pureeing them in a food processor to create a thick paste.

In a medium mixing bowl, beat the egg thoroughly. Add milk and oil and beat again. Stir in chick pea flour or paste until the mixture becomes a thin paste (you should be able to pour it now). Stir half of the blueberries into the mixture. Ladle spoonfuls into a well-oiled, heated skillet (oil should just be starting to make ripples). Turn pancakes when the edges are brown and bubbles start to pop through the center of the pancake. Add oil to the skillet as needed. Sweeten the stacks of pancakes with the fresh blueberries, yogurt, maple syrup, raw honey, blueberry jam or the sweetener or your choice.

Heart-Warming Sweet Potato Pancakes
by David Richard, Ridgefield, CT

These pancakes are tasty, satisfying and free of most common allergens!
Use the many variations to appeal to everyone's tastes and to keep the
recipe evolving.

Vegetarian, wheat-free, corn-free, heart smart

Makes a dozen 3- to 4-inch pancakes

> *2/3 cup of brown rice (may substitute buckwheat) flour*
> *1 cup rice, soy or almond milk*
> *1 medium to large sweet potato, steamed and well mashed*
> *1 large egg*
> *1 tablespoon expeller-pressed oil*
> *1/2 teaspoon gluten-free baking powder*

In a medium mixing bowl, beat the egg thoroughly. Add milk and oil
and beat again. Stir in the mashed sweet potato (lump-free) and flour
until the mixture becomes a thin paste (you should be able to pour it
now). Ladle spoonfuls into a well-oiled, heated skillet (oil should just be
starting to ripple). Turn pancakes when the edges are brown and add oil
to the skillet as needed. Add sweet "fixins" from the list below—or create
your own!

Sweet "fixins":

> *pure maple syrup (warmed) with ground pecans*
> *Medjool date pieces sprinkled on goat's or sheep's yogurt*
> *apple sauce or apple-berry sauce*
> *chopped bananas on goat's or sheep's yogurt*
> *baked apples with juices (add warmed apple juice as needed)*
> *warm rum with stewed raisins*
> *pineapple marinade (slowly cooked fresh pineapple in pineapple or apple juice, pureed)*
> *whole precooked wild rice may be added to give a heartier flavor and texture*
> *(Add warming spices such as cinnamon, nutmeg, clove and ginger—as the spirit moves you.}*

New Salem Buckwheat Pancakes

by Ziporah Hildebrandt, www.ravensridge.bookworks.com, Shutesbury, MA

Vegan, wheat-free, corn-free, heart smart, low fat

These vegan pancakes were popular at the New Salem Restaurant in New Salem, Massachusetts.

> *1 1/2 cups buckwheat flour*
> *1 1/2 cups brown rice flour*
> *2 1/2 teaspoons baking powder*
> *1/2 teaspoon salt*
> *2–2 1/2 cups soy or rice milk*
> *oil for the griddle*

In a bowl, combine buckwheat flour, brown rice flour, baking powder, and salt. Add 2–2 1/2 cups soy or rice milk to make slightly thick batter.* Drop large spoonfuls of batter onto a hot oiled pan. Cooks well at medium-low heat. Turn when no longer liquid in center.

*A thicker batter that holds to a spoon makes pancakes that are high and soft when hot, and chewy when cold, suitable for spreading nut butter. Thinner batter makes the more traditional breakfast pancake. These pancakes freeze well and can be reheated easily in a toaster oven. Just let them cool thoroughly before packing in freezer bag.

Gluten-free Pancakes

by Denise Roseland, Lakewinds Natural Foods, Minnetonka, MN

These pancakes also make great mini-pizza crusts or sandwiches when topped with your favorite toppings.

Vegetarian, wheat-free, corn-free, heart smart, low fat

Serves 6

> *1 large egg*
> *1/4 cup maple syrup*
> *2 tablespoons vegetable oil*

1 cup rice milk
2 cups brown rice flour
1 teaspoon baking soda
1/2 teaspoon salt
vegetable oil for frying

Whisk together eggs, maple syrup, oil and rice milk. Mix in flour, baking soda, and salt. Heat oil on large skillet or griddle. Spoon batter onto griddle. When bubbles appear all over the surface of the pancake and edges are set, flip pancakes over. Cook about 1 to 2 minutes on second side or until golden brown. Serve immediately.

Cinnamon Raisin French Toast
by Len Huber, Shutesbury, MA

Serve with yogurt, applesauce, or maple syrup for a divine breakfast. Kids of all ages love this one.

Vegetarian, corn-free, salt-free

Serves 3–4
Time: 15 minutes

10 slices cinnamon raisin sourdough bread
2 eggs scrambled
1/2 cup vanilla soy milk
1 teaspoon cinnamon
2 teaspoons honey
2 teaspoons vanilla
1 tablespoon canola oil

In a large mixing bowl, scramble the eggs. Mix in soy milk, cinnamon, honey and vanilla. Dip bread slices in the bowl. Flip them over to make sure batter covers both sides. Heat a large skillet or griddle. Add oil. When oil is hot, put bread slices on the griddle. Fry for a minute or two. Flip over bread slices. Fry for another minute or two till bread is brown on both sides.

Spectacular Oatmeal
by Len Huber, Shutesbury, MA

Hearty and warming, this is a sweet porridge perfect for a chilly morning.

Vegan, heart smart, wheat-free, corn-free, low fat, salt-free

Serves 4–6

> *7 cups water*
> *1 teaspoon ginger, finely chopped*
> *1 tablespoon cinnamon*
> *1/4 cup almonds, chopped*
> *1/3 cup raisins*
> *1 apple*
> *1 1/2 cups oatmeal*

Put water in pot on high heat. Chop ginger and add to pot. Sprinkle cinnamon over the surface of the water. Chop almonds and add, dice apple and add, then add raisins. When water comes to a boil, reduce to low simmer and add oatmeal. Simmer for about 30 minutes, stirring occasionally.

Daddy's Waffles
by Len Huber, Shutesbury, MA

These waffles, made with lots of vanilla, are a sweet treat for kids of all ages.

Vegetarian, corn-free, low fat

Serves 4–6

> *1 egg*
> *1 1/2 cups whole wheat pastry flour*
> *3 tablespoons baking powder*
> *1/2 teaspoon sea salt*
> *2/3 cup rice milk*
> *1/2 cup apple juice*

3 tablespoons canola oil + 1 tablespoon for the waffle iron
3 tablespoons vanilla
3 tablespoons arrowroot

Heat up your waffle iron. Scramble the egg in a large bowl. Add and mix all the other ingredients together. When the waffle iron is hot, brush on 1 tablespoon of oil. Ladle in some batter. Let waffle cook for four minutes. Remove and serve with your favorite topping: maple syrup, yogurt, or apple sauce. Repeat till you use up all the batter.

English Muffin Loaves
by Ziji Beth Goren, Shutesbury, MA

Serve with fresh whipped butter and your favorite jam. (Liquid amounts may vary according to your choice of flour.)

Vegetarian, corn-free

Makes 2 loaves

2 packages yeast
6 cups whole wheat or spelt flour
1 tablespoon maple syrup
2 teaspoon salt
2 cups milk
1/4 teaspoon baking soda
1/2 cup water
cornmeal

Preheat the oven to 400 degrees. Combine 3 cups flour, yeast, maple syrup, salt and baking soda in a large mixing bowl. Heat water and milk until very warm (120–130 degrees F). Add to dry mixture, beat well. Stir in rest of flour to make a stiff batter. Spoon into two 8 1/2-inch × 4 1/2-inch pans that have been greased and sprinkled with cornmeal. Sprinkle tops with cornmeal. Cover, let rise in warm place 45 minutes. Bake for 25 minutes. Remove from pans immediately and cool.

Best Banana Muffins
by Lynn Stafford, Vitamin Expo, San Antonio, Texas

Enjoy these sweet muffins for breakfast, snacks and dessert.

Vegetarian, corn-free, wheat-free
Makes 1 dozen muffins

> *1/4 cup oil such as canola or corn oil*
> *1/4 cup applesauce*
> *1/4 cup honey*
> *2 eggs*
> *2 medium bananas, mashed*
> *1 3/4 cup spelt flour*
> *1 teaspoon cinnamon*
> *1 teaspoon baking soda*
> *1/4 cup yogurt (nonfat)*
> *Optional: 1 cup chopped pecans*
> *1/2 cup chocolate or carob chips*

Preheat oven to 350 degrees. Beat oil, applesauce, and eggs until light and fluffy. Stir in bananas. Stir in flour and baking soda. Add and stir in yogurt, pecans and chocolate chips. Oil a muffin tin or insert cupcake liners. Pour in batter and bake for 30 minutes, or until an inserted toothpick comes out clean. Enjoy!

Portabella Mushroom Omelet with Goat Cheese
by Ann Starbare, Crystal Brook Farm, Sterling, MA

You can make this omelet with wine or water; either way it's delicious.

Vegetarian, wheat-free, corn-free

Serves 2

3 tablespoons butter
1 medium onion, diced
1 bell pepper, preferably red or yellow
1 portabella mushroom, diced
6 eggs (3 for each omelet)
1/4 cup water or white wine
4 ounces chevre (goat cheese–2 ounces for each omelet)
2 tablespoons fresh basil (1 teaspoon dried)

Sauté onions and peppers in 1 tablespoon butter for about 3 minutes. Add mushroom and continue cooking until vegetables are soft and tender, about 5 minutes. Set aside.

Beat eggs with water. Heat omelet pan until very hot. Melt a small amount of butter and pour in half of the egg mixture. Use spatula to lift cooked egg from bottom of pan so that liquid eggs will set better. When eggs begin to set, place half the vegetable mixture over half of the cooking eggs. Top vegetable mixture with half the chevre and half the basil. Continue cooking until bottom is brown and eggs are set. Carefully fold half of the eggs over the half with vegetables and goat cheese. Cook a few seconds more and carefully take the omelet out of pan onto serving plate. Repeat with second omelet. ENJOY!!!

Vegetable Tofu Scramble
by Leslie Cerier, Amherst, MA

Like scrambled eggs, tofu is terrific sautéed with veggies and served with tea and toast.

Vegan, wheat-free, corn-free, low fat, heart smart

Serves 4

1 tablespoon extra-virgin olive oil
1 small-medium onion, sliced (1/4 cup)
1 teaspoon turmeric
1 zucchini or yellow squash, sliced (1 1/2 cups)
1 stalk celery, sliced (1/3 cup)
1 tablespoon tamari

1 pound soft tofu or firm, bite-sized cubes
3 tablespoons nutritional yeast
Optional: garnish with chives or scallions

Heat a large skillet. Add oil, onions and turmeric. Sauté 2–3 minutes. Add zucchini and celery. Sauté 2–3 minutes. Add tamari, tofu, and nutritional yeast. Sauté for 3–5 minutes. Taste and adjust the seasonings.

Organic Harvest Fruit Salad
by John Brocek, New England Natural Bakers Inc., South Deerfield, MA

Here is a quick and easy snack that is great for breakfast, too.

Vegetarian, wheat-free, corn-free

Serves 1–2

Choose 3 or 4 of the following and cut into bite-sized pieces:

2 bananas
2 oranges
2 apples
1/2 cup raisins
2 peaches
2 pears
1 cup strawberries
1 cup grapes

Dressing:
1 cup yogurt
1/2 cup fruit juice
1 teaspoon cinnamon or nutmeg
6 ounces cream cheese or 2 tablespoons tahini

1 cup of your favorite trail mix or granola

Choose your fruits and put them in a mixing bowl. Mix dressing ingredients together in a blender. Toss cut fruit with dressing and top with your favorite trail mix.

2

APPETIZERS

Lemon Walnut Bean Paté
by Leslie Cerier, Amherst, MA

This rich, nutty dip is great for a party or snack served with pita bread, olives, carrot and celery sticks. Its texture is thick like a paté.

Vegan, wheat-free, corn-free, heart smart, low fat

Makes: 4 1/2 cups

> *4 cups cooked or canned navy beans*
> *OR start from scratch with 2 cups dried navy beans, presoaked, rinsed and simmered in 6 cups water for 1 1/2 hours*
> *3 scallions, sliced*
> *6 cloves garlic, peeled*
> *1 lemon, juiced, or 1/3 cup lemon juice*
> *1 teaspoon sea salt*
> *2/3 cup walnuts*
> *2 tablespoons chopped fresh dill + several sprigs for garnish*
> *1 5-ounce jar of olives, such as garlic-stuffed olives, for a garnish*

Place cooked beans, scallions, garlic, lemon juice, salt, walnuts and dill in work bowl of food processor. Puree until smooth. Taste and adjust seasonings. Scrape dip into serving bowl, and garnish with olives and dill.

Cool and Spicy Black Bean Dip
by Leslie Cerier, Amherst, MA

This tasty dip is simple to make and gets plenty of flavor from salsa and fresh cilantro. Use mild, medium or hot salsa, whichever you like. You can also always add more cayenne, ground hot pepper, for a hotter dip.

Vegan, wheat-free, corn-free

Makes 6 cups

> *4 cups cooked or canned black beans*
> *Or start from scratch with 2 cups dried black beans soaked overnight and 1 strip kelp and 6 cups water*

2 1/2 cups mild salsa
1 bunch cilantro, 1 1/2 cups leaves
1 bunch scallions, sliced, (1 1/2 cups)
1 teaspoon sea salt or to taste
Optional: add 1/4 teaspoon cayenne for a hotter dip

If starting from scratch, simmer black beans, water and kelp for 1 1/2 to 2 hours.

Rinse the cilantro and twist off and discard the stems. Put the cooked beans and all the other ingredients in a food processor except for a few sprigs of cilantro, which you can use later as a garnish. Blend and taste the dip. Add cayenne for a spicier taste.

Sushi Balls
by Olivia Tacelli, Arlington, MA

Here is an easy way to enjoy vegetarian sushi with the added twist of roasted seeds.

Vegan, low fat, wheat-free, corn-free, heart smart

Makes about 24 balls

1 3/4 cups sweet brown rice
3 1/2 cups boiling water
pinch of sea salt
4 tablespoons mirin (sweet rice wine vinegar)
8 sheets toasted nori, minced with scissors or a sharp knife
8 scallions, sliced into very thin rounds
1 cup grated carrot
1/2 cup minced pickled ginger
3/4 cup toasted sesame seeds (spread raw seeds on a cookie sheet and bake in 350-degree oven 15 minutes)
3/4 cup toasted sunflower seeds (same as above but for 20 minutes . . . use separate pans)

Sauce:
3/4 cup tamari
1 tablespoon sesame oil

1/4 cup mirin
2 tablespoons water
1 tablespoon powdered wasabi (optional)
Optional: shredded lettuce, grated daikon, sliced radish, mung bean sprouts

Boil 3 1/2 cups water, add 1 3/4 cups sweet brown rice and a pinch of salt, cover and reduce heat to medium-low, cook for 1 hour, checking after 45 minutes to make sure there is enough water left to cook the rice, when done. Spread onto a cookie sheet to cool. (Makes 4 cups cooked sweet brown rice.)

Mix 4 tablespoons mirin into the hot cooked rice on the cookie sheet. When rice is cool enough to handle, transfer to a large bowl and mix in nori, scallions, carrot and pickled ginger. Using hands or an ice cream scoop, roll into balls (about 1/4 cup rice mix per ball).

Process toasted seeds in a food processor or blender until they are crumbly. Put seeds in a shallow bowl. Roll the sushi balls in the seeds to coat them.

To make sauce, combine all the ingredients listed in a bowl.

Serve sushi balls on a bed of shredded lettuce/grated daikon/radish/mung bean sprouts. Then spoon sauce over each ball on your own plate.

Wild Mushroom Bruschetta
by Vanessa Paulman, Amherst, MA

Vegetarian, corn-free

Serves 4

I like to cook with wild mushrooms, and while this recipe calls for the Hericium coralloides (coral tooth mushroom), you can easily substitute white button, portobello, crimini or oyster mushrooms.

Coral tooth or Hericium coralloide mushroom tastes almost sweet and looks like a beautiful pure white tuft of iciclelike spines. The stout branches grow from a thick rooting base, sprouting handlike clusters of tips which have white spines that are about 0.5 cm–4 cm long. It grows on hardwoods, especially beech and maple. It is widely distributed, but often grows year after year on the same logs, causing conspicuous white pocket rot. One can usually find it in August through October. This thick, delectable, fruiting body is delicious sautéed, curried or marinated.

1/2 pound mushrooms, sliced into small pieces: your choice of domestic or wild mushrooms: coral tooth, white button mushrooms, portobello, crimini, or oyster.
1/2 teaspoon fresh basil
3 tablespoons butter
1/2 teaspoon thyme
1 large tomato, chopped
1 teaspoon dry sherry
1 teaspoon tamari
8–10 slices of toasted French bread

Sauté all the ingredients, except tomato and bread, until mushrooms are soft and even slightly crisp. Toss hot ingredients with chopped tomato. Serve on top of toast as an appetizer or accompaniment to any dish.

Crostini with Goat Cheese and Sun-Dried Tomato Spread
by Deedy Marble, Culinary Educator, Sterling, MA

Goat cheese, sun-dried tomatoes, and olives make a quick and easy crowd-pleasing spread.

Vegetarian, corn-free

Serves 8

11 ounces chevre, crumbled, room temperature
3/4 cup oil-packed, sun-dried tomatoes, chopped and drained
1/2 cup brine-cured black olives, pitted, chopped
5 tablespoons extra-virgin olive oil
2 teaspoons fresh thyme, chopped

1 French baguette, cut diagonally, 1/3-inch-thick slices
Optional: sprigs of fresh herbs

Mix goat cheese, tomatoes, olives, 1 tablespoon olive oil and thyme in large bowl. Season with salt and pepper. This spread can be made one day ahead. Cover and refrigerate.

Preheat oven to 350 degrees. Arrange bread on baking sheets. Brush with 4 tablespoons olive oil. Bake until lightly toasted, about 10 minutes. Cool, if desired. Transfer spread to serving bowl. Place on platter. Surround with toasts and sprigs of fresh herbs, if desired.

Eggplant Puree

by Stacy Salisbury, Mother Earth's Pantry, Hanoven, PA

Here's a delicious blend of Italian vegetables cooked in olive oil and pureed like a Babaghanoush. Serve over toasted rosemary bread, Italian bread, or Italian crackers. Enjoy.

Vegan, wheat-free, corn-free

Makes 6 cups

> *extra-virgin olive oil*
> *1 large Vidalia onion, sliced*
> *2 cloves garlic, sliced*
> *1 large eggplant, cubed*
> *4 plum red tomatoes*
> *6 white button mushrooms, sliced*
> *1 lemon*
> *1 bunch fresh basil*

In a large skillet, sauté onion and garlic in olive oil over medium heat for 5 minutes. Add eggplant and olive oil as needed until eggplant is fully cooked. Stir in mushrooms, basil, tomatoes, the juice of one lemon. Cover and simmer for 5 minutes. Blend mixture in a food processor or blender on low for a few seconds.

Nori Tempura

by Larch Hanson, Maine Seaweed Company, Steuben, ME

Wild nori, also known as laver, is chopped up into slurry, and then dried out to a thin paper used to make sushi nori. Here is a tasty recipe using wild nori.

Vegan, corn-free, low fat, heart smart

Serves 4–6

> *1 cup whole wheat pastry flour*
> *2 tablespoons arrowroot*
> *1 cup water*

pinch of sea salt
safflower oil
1-ounce package wild nori or laver

Dipping sauce:
1 tablespoon tamari
1 tablespoon water or kombu stock
1 teaspoon mirin
a touch of ginger

Combine flour, arrowroot, water and sea salt. Keep cool until ready to use.

Heat 2 to 3 inches of oil in a wok. The oil is ready when batter dropped into the oil sinks and rises quickly. Break off small bite-sized pieces of nori, dip them in the batter, then into the hot oil. Fry until golden brown and keep warm in a 150-degree oven.

Make a dipping sauce by combining tamari, water, mirin and ginger. Taste and adjust seasonings, if desired.

3

VEGETARIAN
MAIN
COURSES

Golden Quinoa with Yellow Peppers
by Leslie Cerier, Amherst, MA

Here is a beautiful supper in 15 minutes with quinoa, the only grain that is a complete protein. Tomatoes, peppers and thyme make this a very tasty dish.

Vegan, wheat-free, corn-free, heart smart

Serves 4

> *1 cup quinoa, rinsed*
> *2 cups boiling water*
> *1 tablespoon extra-virgin olive oil*
> *1 leek, sliced (1 cup)*
> *2 cloves garlic, sliced*
> *1 yellow tomato or plum tomato, diced (2/3 cup)*
> *1 yellow or red pepper, sliced (2/3 cup)*
> *1/4 teaspoon dried thyme*
> *pinch of sea salt*

Rinse quinoa in a strainer and set aside, allowing excess water to drain into the sink. (You can rinse it in the morning and cook it later in the day, or simply rinse and drain while you slice the vegetables.) Boil water. Sauté leek, garlic, tomatoes, pepper, thyme and salt in olive oil for 5 minutes. Stir in quinoa. Turn off heat. Add boiling water. Resume heat and simmer for 5 minutes or until all the water is absorbed.

Red Chile, Mole Enchilada Casserole
by Peggy Loftfield, Shutesbury, MA

This Santa Fe-style mole (pronounced mo'-lay) is fun to make and has a wonderful, slightly spicy taste!

Vegetarian, wheat-free

Serves 6

> *2 cans precooked pinto beans, drained*

Or to cook beans from scratch, presoak 2 cups (1 pound) dried pinto beans overnight, covered in water. Rinse, then cook in 6 cups water, covered on low heat for 3 hours.

Sauce:
> 2 1/2 tablespoons red chili powder (preferably New Mexican, not cayenne)
> 5 1/2 cups water
> 1/2 teaspoon garlic powder or 3 cloves pressed garlic cloves
> 2 tablespoons cocoa powder, unsweetened
> 5 tablespoons brown rice flour
> 1/2 teaspoon honey
> salt to taste

Simmer 5 cups water, chili powder, and garlic for 1/2 hour in an uncovered saucepan. Whisk occasionally. Mix cocoa powder and brown rice flour with 1/2 cup water. Pour mixture into simmering chili sauce. Keep whisking slowly while sauce bubbles and thickens for 15 minutes. Turn heat to very low, and continue to whisk occasionally till texture is smooth/shiny, adding a little water if needed.

Enchilada:
> 12 corn tortillas (white or blue)
> 6 teaspoons olive oil
> 1–1 1/2 cups grated sharp white cheddar cheese
> 3/4 cup pine nuts, (Pinion from New Mexico, if possible)

In heavy frying pan, lightly crisp fry 12 corn tortillas, one at a time, in 1/2 teaspoon hot olive oil. After quickly turning tortilla over in the oil with a spatula to coat both sides, cook both sides approximately one minute per side over medium heat. Set them on plate covered with a paper towel after cooking to drain excess oil and cool.

Preheat oven to 350 degrees. In a 9-inch × 12-inch × 3-inch casserole dish, ladle and spread 3 large cooking spoonfuls of sauce into the bottom of the casserole dish. Place 2 tortillas on sauce. With slotted cooking spoon, draining off most of the bean juice, spread 1 spoonful of beans on each tortilla. Sprinkle 1/4 of grated cheese around on top of bean layer. Top each tortilla layer with 1 large spoon of sauce. Repeat layers of tortilla, beans, cheese, sauce till tortillas are used up. Spread remaining sauce over top layer. Sprinkle pine nuts over top. Bake for about 15 minutes, till cheese melts and sauce is bubbly. Cool 5 minutes before serving.

Variations:
1. Use boiled or baked, boned chicken pieces with, or instead of, beans.
2. Thickly spread 6 ounces goat cheese mixed with 6 ounces ricotta cheese on tortillas. Cover with sauce, cheddar, and pine nuts. Serve beans/brown rice on the side.
3. Add a layer of sautéed onions, and/or sautéed zucchini.

Black-eyed Peas with Spinach and Herbs
by Nava Atlas, Hudson Valley, NY

(Khoreshe Gormeh Sabzi) Sabzi is the Persian word that refers to greens and herbs, ingredients so typical to this cuisine. This sabzi stew is made with several other characteristic ingredients: Black-eyed peas, a few members of the onion family, plus lemon, cinnamon and nutmeg for flavoring.

Vegan, wheat-free, corn-free, low fat

Serves 4

> 2 tablespoons canola oil
> 1 medium onion, chopped
> 1 cup chopped leek (white part only), well rinsed
> 10 to 12 ounces fresh spinach, stemmed and well rinsed
> 1/2 cup fresh parsley, chopped
> 4 scallions, sliced
> 16-ounce can black-eyed peas, drained and rinsed
> juice of 1/2 to 1 lemon, to taste
> 1/2 teaspoon ground cinnamon
> 1/4 teaspoon ground nutmeg
> salt and freshly ground pepper to taste
>
> hot cooked brown rice
> plain low-fat yogurt for topping, optional

Heat the oil in an extra-large skillet or a steep-sided stir-fry pan. Add the onion and sauté over medium heat until translucent, about 3 to 4 minutes. Add the leek and sauté another 5 minutes or so, until it and the onion are golden. Add the spinach, parsley, and scallion. Cover and steam just until the spinach is wilted, then stir in the black-eyed peas, lemon juice, and spices. Cook just until completely heated through, then season to taste with salt and pepper. Serve at once over hot cooked brown rice, topping each serving with a small amount of yogurt, if desired.

Pasta Ratatouille with Purple Basil and Goat Cheese
by Nava Atlas, Hudson Valley, NY

Purple basil is an eye-catching addition to this classic French stew. Served over pasta and garnished with goat cheese, it becomes a satisfying summer main dish to be served warm or at room temperature.

Corn-free

Serves 4–6

2 tablespoons extra-virgin olive oil
1 cup chopped leeks
2 cloves garlic, minced
1 medium eggplant, peeled and diced
2 medium zucchinis, sliced
1 medium red bell pepper, diced
6 medium ripe, juicy tomatoes, chopped (about 1 1/2 pounds)
1 teaspoon paprika
1/4 cup chopped fresh parsley
1 teaspoon fresh thyme leaves

10–12 ounces pasta, small shapes such as shells or small twists
12 fresh purple basil leaves (use standard green basil if unavailable)
4–6 ounces crumbled goat cheese

salt and freshly ground pepper, to taste

Heat the oil in a soup pot or steep-sided stir-fry pan. Sauté the leeks and garlic over medium-low heat until garlic becomes fragrant, about 2 minutes. Add the eggplant and 4 cups water and bring to simmer. Reduce heat, cover and simmer for 5 minutes. Add the zucchini, bell pepper, tomatoes and paprika. Simmer until vegetables are tender, about 15 to 20 minutes.

When the vegetable mixture is done, remove from heat, stir in the fresh herbs and season to taste with salt and pepper. If time allows, let stand for up to two hours before serving to allow flavors to develop. Before serving, gently reheat, or simply serve at room temperature.

About 15 to 20 minutes before serving, cook the pasta in rapidly simmering water until it is al dente, then drain. Serve by placing a bed of pasta on each serving plate, followed by a generous helping of the stew. Sprinkle purple basil and goat cheese over each serving.

Herbed Goat Cheese-filled Pasta with Roasted Red Pepper Sauce
by Deedy Marble, Culinary Educator, Sterling, MA

These are super!

Corn-free

Serves 8

> 8 manicotti pasta shells, cooked
> nonstick vegetable spray
> 4 red bell peppers
> 1/2 teaspoon freshly ground black pepper
> 1 teaspoon extra-virgin olive oil

Filling:
> 1 small yellow onion, diced
> 1 clove garlic, minced
> 1 1/4 cup cottage cheese
> 3 ounces chevre (goat cheese)
> 1/4 cup finely chopped Italian parsley
> 2 tablespoons finely chopped fresh chives

> *Optional: garnish with toasted pine nuts*

Preheat oven to 400 degrees. Cook manicotti shells according to directions on package. Set aside.

Roast peppers over a gas flame or in a broiler oven, turning to char on all sides. Transfer to a plastic bag and let stand for 10 minutes to steam the skins from the peppers. Rub off blackened skins, remove seeds and stems, and chop peppers coarsely. Transfer to blender and puree with half the ground black pepper and the olive oil. Set aside.

To prepare the filling, coat a nonstick skillet with vegetable spray and warm over medium heat. Add onions and sauté until translucent. Stir in garlic and cook just long enough to release flavor, about 30 seconds. Remove from heat.

In a mixing bowl, combine the onion mixture, cottage cheese, goat cheese, parsley, chives, and remaining pepper. Stir well until thoroughly combined. Fill each pasta shell with 3 tablespoons of the cheese mixture. Place in a shallow baking dish just large enough to hold all 8 shells snugly. Pour pepper sauce over shells and also into the edges of the dish so the shells will not dry out during cooking. Bake for about 25 minutes, or until the sauce bubbles.

Tempeh Sloppy Joe
by Olivia Tacelli, Arlington, MA

A tangy BBQ-style ragout, delicious served with cornbread, bread or rolls, sautéed collard greens, steamed corn or corn grits.

Vegan, corn-free, heart smart, low fat

6 servings

> 4 tablespoons olive oil
> 1 yellow onion, diced (1 cup)
> 1 green bell pepper, diced
> 1 red bell pepper, diced
> 6 cloves garlic, minced
> 2 teaspoons salt
> 3/4 cup ketchup
> 3 tablespoons prepared mustard
> 1 cup crushed or diced ripe tomatoes, canned is fine
> 1/4 cup tamari
> 1/4 cup honey
> 1/4 cup brown rice or apple cider vinegar
> 1 cup water, orange juice or apple juice
> 1 pound tempeh cut into small cubes
> 1/4 cup safflower or sesame oil
> 1/3 cup dry cous cous

Sauté onion, peppers, garlic and salt in the olive oil. Add ketchup, mustard, tomatoes, tamari, honey, vinegar, water or juice. Simmer over medium-low heat, stirring often for 30 minutes.

Heat safflower oil in a wide, heavy-bottomed fry pan till it becomes very hot, about 15 seconds. Add and sauté tempeh till golden brown. Drain tempeh on a brown paper bag. Add to veggie sauce with cous cous, which will cook as it absorbs liquid. Stir well. Add water if it's too thick. This should be thick enough to serve on a plate without running all over.

Marinated Tempeh Kebobs

by Dongmee K. Smith, Four Chimneys Farm Winery, Himrod, NY

Healthy, tasty, and attractive, these kabobs are wonderful, and sure to please both vegans and meat eaters.

Vegan, wheat-free, corn-free, heart smart, low fat

> 1 1/2 pounds (3 8-ounce packages) tempeh
> 1–2 red, yellow or green peppers
> 1 large onion
> 1/2 pound mushrooms
> skewers

Marinade
> 1 cup soy sauce or tamari
> 1 cup semidry white wine
> 12 cloves garlic
> 2 tablespoons olive oil
> 1/4 teaspoon coriander seeds, ground or crushed
> 1/4 teaspoon marjoram, crushed
> freshly ground pepper to taste

Place tempeh slabs in a large steamer, if possible, or cut in large pieces to fit into the steamer. Steam for 20 minutes. Then cut tempeh into 1-inch cubes.

Mix up all the marinade ingredients. Put tempeh in a container that has a cover. Pour marinade over tempeh, cover and refrigerate for 10 to 20 minutes, occasionally turning over the tempeh.

Cut peppers into 1-inch squares and onions into 1- to 2-inch chunks. Rinse mushrooms or brush off any dirt they may have. Place tempeh and vegetables on the skewers, starting with the tempeh, and ending with the pepper. (Example: tempeh, mushroom, onion, pepper, leaving space between each and then repeat the combination, till there is no more room on the skewer.)

Heat a grill or broiler. Make sure the grill is well greased. As you grill or broil the skewers, brush marinade evenly on every side. Grill a few minutes on each side.

Fabulous Lentil Stew
by Leslie Cerier, Amherst, MA

Fennel adds a sweet touch to lentils and vegetables in this thick and hearty stew.

Vegan, wheat-free, corn-free, low fat, heart smart

Serves 6–8

> *1 1/2 cups brown lentils, rinsed*
> *6 cups water*
> *2 bay leaves*
> *1 tablespoon dried nettles, optional*
> *1 strip dulse*
> *1 tablespoon extra-virgin olive oil*
> *5 cloves garlic, sliced*
> *1/4 teaspoon fennel seeds*
> *1 large onion, 1 1/2 cup sliced onions*
> *2–3 stalks celery, sliced (1 1/2 cups)*
> *1 yellow squash, sliced in 1/4-inch quarters (2 cups)*
> *1 bunch kale, sliced (4 cups)*
> *1 pound tomatoes or 1 14-ounce can of diced tomatoes*
> *1/2 teaspoon fresh rosemary or 1/4 teaspoon dried*
> *2 teaspoons fresh thyme or 1 teaspoon dried*
> *1 teaspoon sea salt or to taste*

Boil and simmer the lentils, bay leaves, dulse and nettles for 15 minutes while you sauté the vegetables.

Heat a heavy skillet. Add olive oil, garlic, fennel seeds and onions. Sauté for 5 minutes and add celery. Sauté for 5 minutes and add yellow squash. Sauté for 3 minutes or until it becomes bright yellow. Add fresh chopped kale and sautéed vegetables to the lentils. Simmer for 10 minutes or until the lentils are soft. Add tomatoes. Simmer for a couple of minutes. Add herbs and sea salt. Simmer 2 minutes to blend the flavors and taste. Add more seasonings, if desired.

Tofu Broccoli Quiche
by Marie Summerwood, Syracuse, NY

Treat yourself to this wonderful quiche.

Serves 6–8

Corn-free, wheat-free option

> *3 tablespoons butter*
> *4 cups diced onions*
> *2 pounds tofu*
> *2 cloves garlic, minced*
> *2 teaspoons dried rosemary*
> *1/2 cup whole wheat flour or rice flour*
> *4 cups broccoli florets, partially cooked*
> *1/2 cup tahini*
> *1/2 cup water more or less*
> *1/2 teaspoon sea salt*
> *4 tablespoons tamari or to taste*
> *1 cup walnut or pecan halves*

Preheat oven to 350 degrees. Melt butter in heavy skillet and sauté garlic and onions until translucent. Crush and add rosemary and sauté another minute or so. Crumble the tofu with your fingers or mash with a fork until it is the consistency of creamy cottage cheese. Add this to the flour, tahini, sea salt, tamari and water. Mix this with the onions and fold in most of the broccoli, saving out enough florets for arranging on top.

Transfer to an oiled 13-inch × 9-inch × 2-inch pan and arrange the remaining broccoli and nut halves. Cover and bake 30 minutes. Uncover and bake another 20 minutes or until lightly golden.

Asparagus, Leek, Flax and Sunflower Tart
by French Meadows Bakery and Café, Minneapolis, MN

This tart makes a stylish spring meal with healthy vegetables, some cheeses, and fresh strawberries. It is delicious, light and filling.

Corn-free

Serves 4

1/8 of a 24-ounce loaf (about 3 large slices) yeast-free flax and sunflower round bread
1 tablespoon + 1 teaspoon olive oil
1 pound asparagus (approximately 16 spears)
1 large leek, rinsed, sliced
8 egg whites
1 cup part skim ricotta cheese
4 ounces low-fat Swiss Cheese
1/2 cup skim milk
1/4 teaspoon ground nutmeg
Optional: 1/2 teaspoon sea salt
1 cup strawberries or melon balls

Preheat the oven to 425 degrees. Use blender or food processor to make breadcrumbs. Empty crumbs into deep-dish pie plate. Drizzle with 1 tablespoon olive oil and mix with hands until crumbs are well moistened. Using fingers, gently pat crumbs to cover bottom of pie plate. Place in hot oven and bake for 8 minutes at 425 degrees or until crust is toasted. Lower oven temperature to 400 degrees.

Bring water to boil in a medium saucepan. Clean and trim asparagus. Blanch asparagus in boiling water for 3 minutes or steam over boiling water until tender and easily cut. Drain, cut into 1-iinch pieces and put into medium mixing bowl.

Quarter, rinse and slice tender white and green parts of leek. Sauté in 1 teaspoon olive oil over medium heat. Reduce heat and cook 4 to 5 minutes. Add to mixing bowl with asparagus.

Mix eggs, ricotta cheese, Swiss cheese, milk and nutmeg in a medium bowl or blender just until blended. Gently stir into bowl with asparagus and leeks. Pour gently into pie plate over toasted breadcrumbs. Bake 40 minutes at 400 degrees until puffed and nicely browned. Let cool ten minutes before slicing. Slice into 4 wedges. Serve warm with melon or strawberries.

Escarole and Beans

by Mary Ellen Salvini, Amherst, MA

This is an everyday recipe that I have made for over 42 years. It isn't fancy, but is very delicious and hearty when accompanied by hot crusty Italian bread dipped in oil and vinegar.

Serves 6–8

Wheat-free, corn-free

> *8 cups chopped escarole (about 2 heads)*
> *3 tablespoons olive oil*
> *1 1/4 cups water*
> *1 large onion*
> *3 cloves minced garlic*
> *salt and pepper to taste*
> *3/4 cup white wine*
> *2 cups cooked cannellini beans*
> *pinch of crushed hot pepper*
> *1 tablespoon extra-virgin olive oil*
> *2 tablespoons parmesan cheese*
> *1 pound of ricotta cheese*
> *Optional: garnish with additional parmesan cheese*

In large pot, sauté chopped onion in 3 tablespoons olive oil till softened, about 5 to 7 minutes. Add the minced garlic and sauté till soft, but not browned. Chop the escarole and put in large pot or bowl with cold salted water for 3 minutes and then lift out and rinse.

Pour wine over the sautéed onion and garlic and then add the salt, pepper and the escarole along with the water and cook about 30 minutes. Add beans, hot pepper flakes and the 1 tablespoon extra-virgin olive oil. Cook about 10 minutes to blend flavors making sure there is still liquid in the pot. Turn off the heat. Stir in 2 tablespoons parmesan cheese.

Ladle into 4 bowls and put ricotta on table for all to add a large spoonful in center. Ricotta can be eaten separately with the dish or mixed through to make a wonderful, creamy, flavorful experience.

Cheesey Eggy Casserole
by Karen Romanowski, Amherst, MA

A favorite with children, and an enjoyable dish with greens and grains. Feel free to use just about any green, grain, or cheese; this recipe is very adaptable.

Serves 4

Wheat-free, corn-free

1 large bunch of greens (or any green vegetable—spinach is our favorite, but
kale, broccoli, collards, arugula and tatsoi have all been enjoyed)
3/4 cup milk
3 eggs (beaten)
1 cup cooked rice (millet, barley, spelt, wheat and rye berries are also good)
1 cup grated sharp cheddar cheese (all cheeses also good, try feta or any favorite)

Preheat oven to 350 degrees. Steam greens lightly. Chop greens. Mix everything (except cheese) together and put into greased shallow baking dish (11-inch × 7-inch works well). Cover top with cheese. Bake for 25 to 35 minutes (until set). Serve hot.

Stir-Fry Brown Rice, Tofu and Veggies
by Deedy Marble, Culinary Educator, Sterling, MA

There isn't anything tricky about this recipe . . . just have everything chopped and ready to go in advance. Also, you could substitute shrimp for tofu.

Serves 4–6

Wheat-free, corn-free, heart smart

3 tablespoons peanut oil
1 bunch green onions, white bulb and tops chopped separately
1 medium sweet potato, peeled, halved lengthwise and sliced thinly
1 small green pepper, cut into thin strips (julienne)
2 medium carrots, thinly sliced
1 zucchini, thinly sliced
2 cups cooked brown rice
1 cup bean sprouts
1 cup fresh mushrooms, sliced (any variety)
1/4 cup honey
1/4 cup low-salt soy sauce
1 pound tofu, cut into small cubes (texture is your choice)
Optional: sprinkle sesame seeds over each serving as a garnish

Heat oil in wok or large heavy skillet. Stir fry white part of scallions, sweet potato, green pepper, carrots and zucchini until BARELY tender. Add cooked rice, sprouts, mushrooms, tops of green onions and small cubes of tofu. Cook briefly, until heated through. Combine honey and soy sauce and pour over mixture. Stir. Serve immediately.

Sweet Potato and Bean Burritos
by Kris H. Bidwell, Florence, MA

Serve with brown rice and a green salad for a healthy meal the whole family will love.

Corn-free, vegan option

Serves 6–8

> *1 large onion*
> *2 cloves garlic*
> *2 tablespoons olive oil*
> *3 medium to large sweet potatoes, peeled and grated*
> *1 tablespoon cumin*
> *2 teaspoons oregano*
> *1/2 teaspoon cayenne (or to taste)*
> *2 15-ounce cans refried pinto or black beans*
> *Optional: 2 cups grated cheddar cheese*
> *salt and pepper to taste*
> *12 10-inch flour tortillas*
> *sour cream*
> *salsa*

Preheat oven to 350 degrees. Sauté onion and garlic in oil until onion is translucent. Add grated sweet potato and seasonings, stir. Cook covered for 15 minutes or until sweet potatoes are tender. Mix in two cans of beans, and, if desired, add cheese too.

Spoon mixture onto open tortillas and roll up (it is easier to roll if you spoon onto the middle of the left third of the tortilla and roll towards the right). Place burritos into greased 9-inch × 13-inch pan. Cover with tinfoil and bake 25 minutes or until insides are hot.

Serve burritos topped with salsa and sour cream.

Creamy Mushroom Tempeh
by Kemper Carlsen, Shutesbury, MA

A very rich, satisfying dish and excellent introduction to how savory tempeh can be. Delicious served over whole wheat flat noodles or long grain brown rice.

Vegan option, heart smart, corn-free

Serves 4–6

> 12 ounces tempeh
> 1/2 medium onion, cut into thin slivers
> 1 pound shiitake mushrooms cut into thin slivers
> 4 tablespoons canola oil
> 3 tablespoons tamari (or use less to taste)
> 1 1/4 cups water
> 1 teaspoon salt
> 1 teaspoon dry mustard
> 1/2 teaspoon dill
> 1/4 teaspoon white pepper
> 1 cup tofu sour cream* or 1 cup sour cream

Cut tempeh into 2-inch long strips, 1/2 inch wide. Fry gently in a large cast-iron pan with 2 tablespoons oil till lightly brown on both sides (some folks like the tempeh heavily fried with more oil). Remove tempeh and set aside.

In same large pan, add 2 tablespoons oil, and sauté onion and mushrooms till onions are translucent and mushrooms well cooked. Add dill and white pepper and sauté a couple of minutes longer. Add tempeh to onions and mushrooms and sauté for 5 minutes.

Dissolve mustard, tamari and salt in water and add to pan. Simmer for 5 to 10 minutes, stirring gently until most of liquid is absorbed. Add more water if needed so that tempeh is juicy.

*Tofu Sour Cream:
A nice alternative to the dairy variety. Creamy and mild.

Vegan, heart smart, low fat

Makes one cup

> *1/2 pound silken or soft tofu*
> *1 tablespoon tamari (use less to taste)*
> *1 teaspoon cider vinegar*
> *1/8 teaspoon onion powder*
> *1/8 teaspoon garlic powder*
> *1/16 teaspoon ground nutmeg*

Blend all ingredients till smooth in a blender or food processor. Right before serving tempeh, gently stir in 1 cup tofu sour cream or dairy sour cream.

Marinated Baked Tofu
by Kemper Carlsen, Shutesbury, MA

Everyone loves this one, even meat eaters, especially when served with a nice vegan shiitake mushroom gravy, mashed potatoes and cooked greens.

Vegan, wheat-free

Serves 5

> *1/8 cup tamari*
> *1/4 cup water*
> *1/8 cup canola or olive oil*
> *1 tablespoon rice vinegar*
> *1 1/2 tablespoons honey*
> *2 teaspoons mustard powder*
> *1 teaspoon garlic powder*
> *1 tablespoon lemon juice*
> *2 tablespoons nutritional yeast*
> *2 1-pound blocks of extra-firm tofu sliced endwise into 5 slices*

Preheat oven to 350 degrees. Whisk together all ingredients but tofu. Lay tofu slices on a large clean kitchen towel, cover with another towel and press gently to take out extra moisture from tofu. Lay one layer of pressed tofu out in pan(s). Cover with the marinade and let sit for an hour or more, turning tofu over a few times. Bake for 1/2 hour to 1 hour, depending on how dry you like your tofu.

Thai Coconut Basil Sauce over Tofu and Vegetables
by Sylvia Brallier, Las Vegas, NV

Folks who claim not to like tofu have not tried this dish. Coconut milk, basil, chili paste, garlic, ginger and lime make this tofu and veggie dish delicious and fragrant.

Vegan

Serves 3–4

Sauce:
> 2 tablespoons toasted sesame oil
> 1 1/2 tablespoons diced garlic
> 1 1/2 tablespoons finely grated fresh ginger
> 1 tablespoon whole wheat flour
> 8 ounces coconut milk
> tamari to taste
> 1/3 of a fresh lime, squeezed
> cayenne pepper or chili paste to the heat level desired
> 1/4 cup fresh basil, coarsely chopped

Sauté the garlic and ginger in the toasted sesame oil. Make a roux by adding the flour to the oil once the garlic and ginger are cooked. Slowly add in the coconut milk and the tamari while stirring. Remove from heat. Add lime, chili paste, and chopped basil. Set aside.

Tofu and Vegetables:
> 1 pound firm tofu, cubed
> 2 tablespoons toasted sesame oil
> 1 1/2 cups broccoli, sliced
> 3/4 cup sliced mushrooms
> 1/2 of a red pepper, sliced
> 20 fresh snow peas
> 1 cup mung bean sprouts

Heat a heavy skillet. Use cast iron, if possible. Add 1 tablespoon of toasted sesame and sauté tofu until browned. Remove from pan and set aside.

Steam broccoli for a few minutes, till bright green. Add snow peas and steam for 2 minutes. Add and steam mung bean sprouts one minute. Remove from heat. Meanwhile, sauté the mushrooms and red peppers in 1 tablespoon toasted sesame oil. Add and stir in sautéed tofu to mushrooms and peppers. Then add steamed vegetables and the sauce. Stir together to mix and warm, and serve over soba noodles or brown rice.

Japanese Breaded Tofu with Red Pepper Lemon Sauce
by Tagan Engel, Brooklyn, NY

Wonderful served with pea shoots or other light greens (such as maché or baby romaine). The red pepper sauce is also delightful as a salad dressing.

Vegan, wheat-free, corn-free

Serves 4

> *12 ounces extra-firm silken tofu**
> *1 1/2 cups cornstarch or arrowroot or rice flour*
> *salt and pepper*
> *oil for frying*

Heat 1 inch of oil in a heavy frying pan. Slice tofu into 1/4-inch rectangles. Season each piece of tofu with salt and pepper.

Coat each piece of tofu in cornstarch just before you are ready to place it in the hot oil. Fry a few pieces at a time, turning as soon as one side is lightly browning.

Place tofu on paper towels to absorb any oil.

Sauce:
> *juice of 2 lemons*
> *2 tablespoons honey*
> *pinch of salt*
> *1/2 cup water*
> *1 finely diced red pepper*
> *garnish with fresh chopped cilantro*

Place lemon juice, honey, salt and water in a pan, simmer to reduce by 1/4, about 3 minutes. Turn off heat and add red pepper. Let sit for 2 minutes.

Drizzle tofu and greens with a few spoonfuls of red pepper sauce. Garnish with cilantro.

*This tofu is best made right before serving, but if necessary, it may be made ahead and reheated in a single layer on foil in a preheated 400-degree oven for 5 minutes or until hot.

Vegetarian Chili

by Lucille Mayer, FVO International Certification Services, Medina, ND

You will not believe that this chili is meatless. It is thick and hearty and perfect for the football weather or winter lunch boxes. For an even richer texture, you can add tempeh, a savory soy product that contributes healthy low-fat protein. Vegetarian chili freezes well. Make extra for easy weekend lunches.

Vegan, wheat-free, corn-free, low fat, heart smart

Serves 6–8

> *1 cup minced onion*
> *1/2 cup minced celery*
> *1/3 cup green bell pepper, minced*
> *1 tablespoon minced garlic*
> *1/2 cup dry red wine*
> *1/2 cup diced canned green chilies*
> *3 cups chopped tomatoes*
> *3 cups cooked pinto beans*
> *2 teaspoons cumin*
> *1 teaspoon chopped cilantro*
> *1 tablespoon cumin powder, or to taste*
> *2 teaspoons dried oregano*
> *2 cups water*
> *3 tablespoons tomato paste*
> *Optional: herbal salt substitute*

In a large stock pot or Dutch oven over medium-high heat, cook onion, celery, bell pepper and garlic in red wine for 10 minutes. Add chilies and tomatoes and cook 3 minutes. Add beans, cumin, cilantro, chili powder, oregano, the water, and tomato paste. Raise heat to high, bring to a boil, then lower heat to medium. Cover pot and cook until chili is thick (45 minutes to 1 hour.) Taste for seasoning, add salt or herb salt, if needed. Serve hot.

Roasted Corn and Pepper Chili

by Ruth Hampton, Oneota Community Food Co-op, Decorah, IA

Roasted peppers and corn make this chili extra special. This dish is nice served with warm corn tortillas or flatbread.

Vegan, wheat-free

Serves 6–8

> 3 cups cooked pinto, kidney beans or anasazi (AKA Jacob's cattle bean)
> 1 cup tomatoes, diced or pureed
> 1 potato, medium size, diced
> 1 sweet potato, small, diced
> 1 onion, chopped
> 3/4 cup sweet corn, roasted, if possible*, or hominy
> 2 cups water
> 1–2 bell peppers, roasted**
> 1 dried New Mexico or Ancho chili, simmered to soften
> 1–2 limes
> 1 teaspoon coriander
> 1 teaspoon cumin
> 1/8 teaspoon ground cloves
> salt and pepper to taste
> Optional: 1 teaspoon powdered carob; more water, spices or tomato

*About roasting corn: If I have a grill going I will partially boil the corn on the cob then place it directly onto the grill until it is browning and slightly dried out. You can also soak the ears in their husks in cold water for 1/2 hour and then grill the corn in a fire or on the BBQ grill until they are cooked. The water helps keep the husks from catching fire. I often make the soup with frozen corn and it tastes great, too. After you have removed the corn from the cob, the roasted cob can make a great soup stock, if you choose to use it.

**About roasting peppers: I lay them directly onto the gas burner so the flame chars the skin until it is black. Turn the pepper until almost all of the skin is charred. Remove from the flame and let cool for a bit. As you rub the skin it should slough off by itself. Do not rinse with water, a few specks of charred skin will help give it the smoky flavor. If you do not have a gas burner they can be grilled on the barbecue grill or simply roasted in a hot oven on a rack on a sheet pan.

Puree the roasted peppers and the soaking dried peppers together. Combine all ingredients except for the lime in a heavy cooking pot and simmer for an hour. Add the lime at the end and adjust the seasonings.

4

MEAT AND
FISH
ENTREES

Italian Shrimp and Vegetable Sauté
by Leslie Cerier, Amherst, MA

Basil, thyme and lots of garlic lend a Mediterranean accent to this main dish. Serve with pasta or a crusty whole wheat loaf.

Wheat-free, dairy-free, corn-free

Serves 4

> *1 tablespoon canola oil*
> *9 cloves organic garlic, sliced*
> *1/4 teaspoon ground cayenne pepper*
> *1 yellow onion, sliced (1 cup)*
> *3 small zucchini, sliced (3 cups)*
> *1/4 pound string beans, sliced (1 1/2 cups)*
> *2 carrots, grated*
> *1 1/2 pounds medium shrimp, peeled and deveined*
> *1/4 cup clam or chicken broth or water*
> *4 teaspoons dried basil*
> *3 teaspoons dried thyme*
> *1/2 teaspoon sea salt or to taste*
> *1/4 teaspoon ground black pepper or to taste*
> *2 tablespoons extra-virgin olive oil*

Heat a wok or heavy skillet for about a minute. Add and swirl canola oil up the sides of the pan till hot and hazy. Add garlic, onion and cayenne. Stir fry for 5 minutes. Add and stir fry zucchini and string beans for 3 minutes. Add grated carrots and stir fry for 1 minute until they turn bright orange. Add shrimp and continue stir frying for 2 to 3 minutes. Add clam juice or other liquid and cover the pan for 3 minutes, or until shrimp curl tightly. Do not overcook. Add dried basil and thyme, salt and pepper. Stir, taste and adjust seasonings if necessary.

Moqueca de Frango
by Tagan Engel, Brooklyn, NY

This Brazilian coconut chicken stew dish may be prepared with whole chicken pieces, any firm fish, shrimp or tofu. It is a traditional dish from Bahia, Brazil, which has its culinary roots in Nigeria.

Wheat-free, dairy-free, corn-free, vegetarian option

Serves 4

4 teaspoons salt
2 tablespoons canola oil
1 medium onion, quartered
3 garlic cloves
1 red bell pepper
1/2 green bell pepper
1 large tomato
2 cans coconut milk
4 boneless chicken breasts, cut into 1/2-inch strips

In a blender or food processor puree 4 teaspoons salt, garlic, onion and canola oil. Remove the seeds and stem from the red and green pepper and cut into large pieces. Quarter the tomato and add it along with the peppers to the food processor. Pulse until you have a fine salsa texture.

Place the coconut milk and salsa mixture into a frying pan with high sides or a sauce pot and simmer partially covered for 25 minutes, stirring occasionally. Add sliced chicken breasts. Stir to separate pieces and simmer uncovered for another 15 minutes, or until chicken is cooked through, and sauce has thickened a bit. Serve over rice.

Thai Noodles with Chicken, Peppers and Caramelized Onion Sauce
by Tagan Engel, Brooklyn, NY

To make this dish with tofu, cut firm tofu into cubes and simmer with onion sauce before adding peppers.

Corn-free, dairy-free, vegetarian option

Serves 4

1 8-ounce package udon or rice udon noodles
6 tablespoons canola oil
2 medium onions, thinly sliced, julienne
2 tablespoons honey
2–3 teaspoons salt, or to taste
2 1/2 cups water

1 yellow pepper julienne
1 red pepper julienne
1 green pepper julienne
zest and juice of 2 limes
3 boneless chicken breasts, sliced into 1/2-inch slices
1/2 cup cilantro leaves, rinsed and chopped

Cook and drain noodles according to instructions on package. Toss noodles with one tablespoon of oil to prevent them from sticking together. Set aside.

Put 4 tablespoons of oil (enough to just cover the bottom of the pan) in a large frying pan set over medium-high heat. Add onions, honey and 2 teaspoons salt. Fry and stir occasionally (so that any browning sections get stirred into the rest of the onions.) When most of the onions have browned and there are brown bits stuck to the pan (5 to 8 minutes) add 1/2 cup water and simmer to dissolve onions. Continue adding more water if it has evaporated and the onions are still intact. Simmer for 4 minutes more until half the onions have dissolved to form the sauce. Add the julienne peppers to the onions and simmer over medium heat until peppers have softened, about 2 minutes. Stir in 2/3 of the lime zest and 2/3 of the lime juice. Taste sauce and add more salt if desired. Pour the onion and pepper sauce over the noodles.

Return the pan to medium high heat, add 2 tablespoons oil. Add chicken to pan and season with salt. Let chicken cook on one side before turning. When chicken is almost done, add the rest of the lime juice and zest. Sauté chicken till cooked through and toss with noodles. Garnish with cilantro and serve.

Maple Rosemary Chicken
with Asparagus and Seared Apples
by Tagan Engle, Brooklyn, NY

This recipe can also be made into a vegetarian dish by substituting small cubes of tofu or seitan for chicken.

Dairy-free, wheat-free, corn-free, vegetarian option

Serves 4

1 1/3 cups water
one bunch asparagus cut into 1 1/2-inch pieces
1 apple cut into 1/8-inch wedges (granny smith, cortland, or other firm apple)

1/4 cup maple syrup
2 teaspoons sea salt
Optional: 1/2 teaspoon pepper
3 tablespoons canola or olive oil
5 stems fresh rosemary, leaves picked and finely chopped
4 boneless chicken breasts cut into 1/2-inch × 2-inch strips

In a frying pan over high heat bring 1 cup of water to a simmer. Add asparagus pieces, cover and cook for 1 minute or until bright green. Immediately remove asparagus with a slotted spoon and plunge into cold water to stop the cooking process. Transfer to a plate when cool.

Toss apple slices with 1 tablespoon maple syrup, a pinch of salt and pepper, 1 tablespoon oil, and 1/4 of the rosemary. Dry frying pan and return to high heat. When pan is hot add 1 tablespoon of oil and a single layer of apples, being careful not to crowd them to avoid steaming. When the bottom of apple slices are brown (1 to 2 minutes), turn them over and brown other side. If any burning begins, either on apples or pan juices, lower the heat a bit. Continue cooking apples in batches until they are all nicely caramelized. Add apples to asparagus.

Toss the chicken with the remaining maple syrup, rosemary, 2 teaspoons salt, 1 tablespoon oil, and 1/2 teaspoon pepper if desired. Over high heat, cook the chicken in 2 batches, much the same way as the apples. Place the chicken pieces in a single layer in the pan, adding 1 tablespoon of oil to the pan for each batch. When the bottom of each piece is dark brown, turn it over. When the juices in the pan begin to get very dark, but before they burn, add 1/3 cup of water to deglaze the pan. Stir the chicken around and scrape up any bits stuck to the pan. Let the juices reduce to a syrup that coats the chicken. Remove chicken from the pan, adding it to the apples and asparagus, and repeat the process with the remaining chicken.

Combine all the ingredients in the frying pan to heat, and serve over rice.

Gaella's Gingery Chicken and Pasta
by Gaella Elnell, South River Miso Company, Inc., Conway, MA

Garlic, ginger, tamari and miso provide the Asian accent for this tasty chicken and pasta dish.

Dairy-free, wheat-free option, corn-free

Serves 4–6

1 pound boneless, skinless chicken breasts (cut into small pieces)

Marinade:
4–5 cloves garlic chopped fine
1 4-inch piece of ginger, peeled and grated
1/2 cup sweet brown rice miso or other light miso
1/2 cup water

1 pound of your favorite pasta, cooked and cooled
2 tablespoons olive or sesame oil
3–4 cups fresh spinach (or other leafy greens), rinsed and chopped
1 tablespoon tamari
1 pinch of black pepper

Blend all marinade ingredients and pour over chicken. Allow chicken to marinate for 1 to 2 hours in refrigerator.

Cook pasta, and rinse in cool water. Set aside.

Heat oil in large pan. Add chicken and cook for 4 to 5 minutes on medium flame. Add spinach and pasta, then tamari and pepper. Serve immediately.

Cajun Fish Stew
by Leslie Cerier, Amherst, MA

Tilapia, also known as Saint Peter's fish, is very lean and tender with a mild flavor. You may also use pollack, monkfish, or catfish as an alternative. This simple and quick-to-prepare stew is mildly spicy.

Dairy-free, wheat-free, corn-free

Serves 4

2 tablespoons canola oil
1 large onion, sliced (1 1/2 cups)
1 head of cauliflower, cut into florets (4 cups)
2 carrots, sliced (1 1/2 cups)
2 1/2 teaspoons cumin powder
1 tablespoon + 2 teaspoons chili powder
1/4 teaspoon cayenne
2 cups water
1 pound Tilapia fillets
1/2 teaspoon sea salt or to taste

Heat canola oil in a heavy stew pot on medium high. Add the onions and sauté for 5 minutes. Add cauliflower, carrots and spices. Sauté for an additional 2 minutes. Add water, stirring to blend. Cover and simmer for 20 minutes or until cauliflower and carrots are tender.

Rinse fish and lay the fillets on top of the vegetables. After 2 minutes gently turn over fish and let it cook for an additional 2 minutes. Cut the fish into bite-sized pieces by stirring it into the stew. Cover and cook for 2 more minutes. Uncover and stir for about 5 minutes, or until fish has turned white and flaky. Taste and adjust the seasonings, if needed.

Grilled Tuna with a Ginger Citrus Sauce
by Leslie Cerier, Amherst, MA

This main dish looks beautiful on a bed of fresh tender greens. It tastes best warm or at room temperature.

Dairy-free, wheat-free, corn-free

Serves 4

Marinade:
1/3 cup lemon juice (1 lemon)
1/3 cup orange juice (1 small orange)
2 tablespoons extra-virgin olive oil
1 tablespoon sesame oil
2 tablespoons tamari
2 heaping tablespoons grated organic ginger
2 cloves organic garlic, sliced

Kebobs:
1 pound tuna steak, cut into 1/2-inch chunks
1 yellow summer squash, sliced into quarters or half-moons (2 1/2 cups)
1 zucchini, sliced into quarters or half-moons (1 1/2 cups)
4 skewers

To make the marinade, combine lemon and orange juices, oils, tamari, garlic and ginger. Put the tuna in a glass bowl, cover with marinade and refrigerate for 20 minutes. Thread both squashes and tuna on four skewers, leaving about 1/2 inch between the vegetables and each piece of tuna. Brush with marinade and broil for 10 minutes.

Barley Lentil Loaf

by George Mandler, Whole Foods for You, Lincoln, MA

Feel free to experiment with different vegetables—maybe add cabbage or burdock. Also, if using sodium-free chicken broth you may need to add more salt, or use umeboshi vinegar in place of salt.

Dairy-free, wheat-free, corn-free

Serves 4–6

> *1 cup hulled barley*
> *1/4 cup red lentils*
> *1/4 cup sunflower seeds*
> *1/3 cup dried shiitake mushrooms, soaked*
> *2 tablespoons olive oil*
> *1 onion, sliced*
> *2–3 carrots, sliced*
> *2 celery stalks, sliced*
> *1/4 teaspoon Celtic sea salt or sea salt*
> *1 tablespoon thyme*
> *1 quart chicken broth (can or asceptic)*
> *Optional: 1/4 cup dry red wine*
> *sprigs of parsley*

Soak barley, lentils and sunflower seeds overnight. This enhances the flavors of the grains and seeds.

Preheat oven to 350 degrees. Soak shiitakes in water to cover. Add 1 tablespoon olive oil to a large skillet, and sauté onions until they become translucent. Add carrots, celery and shiitake. Sauté for 2 minutes and add a pinch of sea salt to seal flavor.

Drain soaking barley, lentils and sunflower seeds. Add them along with the thyme to the vegetables. Sauté for another 2 minutes.

In a large pot, heat chicken broth and wine. Once the broth begins to boil, add the skillet mixture to pot. Stir and simmer for a couple of minutes to blend flavors. Transfer this mixture to an 8-inch × 8-inch glass baking dish, greased with olive oil. Place in oven covered. Uncover after 30 minutes and bake for another 20 minutes. Serve garnished with sprigs of parsley.

Shrimp Kabobs with Honey Mustard Sauce
by Leslie Cerier, Amherst, MA

Serve on top of rice or pasta with a green salad on the side. You could grill or broil these kabobs.

Dairy-free, wheat-free, corn-free

Serves 4
Makes 16 skewers

> 4 tablespoons sesame oil
> 3 tablespoons honey
> 4 tablespoons wet mustard
> 1 tablespoon tamari
> 1 tablespoon maple syrup
> 1 1/4 pounds medium shrimp, shelled, deveined, and rinsed
> 1 green pepper, cut into 1-inch squares
> 1/4 pound mushrooms, sliced in half lengthwise
> 1 zucchini, sliced in rounds
> 1 small red onion, sliced in rounds

To make the marinade, combine oil, honey, maple syrup, mustard and tamari. Taste it and adjust the seasoning if desired. Put the deveined shrimp in a glass bowl, cover with marinade and refrigerate for 15 minutes to 1 hour. Thread mushrooms, zucchini, onions and shrimp on skewers, leaving about 1/2 inch between the vegetables and each shrimp. Put the skewers in a large glass baking dish and pour remaining marinade over the shrimp and vegetables. Broil for 5 to 10 minutes or until shrimp turns orange.

Havana Pork Roast
by Carol Joyce, White Buffalo Herbs, Warwick, MA

When I lived on my 3-masted schooner, I sailed south and discovered the incredible taste of bitter oranges. They really make all the difference in pork. If you can't find them in your neighborhood, you can substitute lime juice and orange juice.

Dairy-free, wheat-free, corn-free

Serves 8–10 if boneless pork is used, if bone in, serves 6–8

> *4 pounds lean loin of pork (any cut can be substituted, but loin has the thickest meat)*
> *1 whole bulb garlic*
> *4 whole bitter oranges (Naranja) or 1 cup Naranja juice (found in Latin section of most groceries)*
> *1/8 teaspoon powdered orange zest*
> *1/8 teaspoon nutmeg (best tasting, if freshly grated)*
> *1/8 teaspoon coarse ground black pepper*
> *Optional: pinch sea salt*

Preheat oven to 325 degrees. Rinse the pork, pat dry. Cut 1/2-inch slashes in the pork, making small pockets that a clove of garlic can hide in. Put a clove of garlic in each "pocket." Squeeze the oranges all over the pork (or pour 1 cup of bottled juice over the roast). Reserve any extra juice that runs off for future basting.

Mix the spices together. Rub the pork all over with spice mixture. Put in roasting pan and cook 20 minutes per pound at 325 degrees, basting occasionally with reserved juices. Let pork sit at room temperature for 10 minutes before slicing.

Herb-Crusted Salmon with Sun-Dried Tomato Sauce
by Dongmee K. Smith, Four Chimneys Farm Winery, Himrod, NY

Gourmet, yet easy to make, these tempting herb crusted salmon fillets look impressive at the dinner table smothered with sun-dried tomato sauce.

Dairy-free, corn-free

Serves 6

For the Dry Rub:
> *1/4 cup dried basil*
> *1/4 cup dried thyme*
> *1/4 cup dried oregano*
> *1 teaspoon crumbled rosemary*

1 tablespoon black peppercorns
1 tablespoon pink peppercorns
1/4 cup whole wheat pastry flour
1 teaspoon sea salt

6 1/2-pound salmon fillets
1/2 cup olive oil

For the Sauce:
1 cup dry white wine
4 sun-dried tomatoes packed in oil, drained, patted dry, and chopped fine*
1 large shallot, chopped fine*
1 tablespoon fresh lemon juice
1 stick (1/2 cup) unsalted butter, cut into bits

Preheat the oven to 400 degree. Prepare the dry rub: In a small bowl stir together the herbs and the peppercorns. In a spice grinder, grind the mixture in batches until it is fine, transferring it as it is ground into another bowl. Add the flour and the salt to the herb mixture. Dredge the salmon in the herb and flour mixture, coating it well. Arrange the salmon on a greased baking sheet, brush it with the oil, and roast it in the middle of the oven for 8 to 10 minutes, or until it is just cooked through.

Make the sauce: In a skillet combine the wine, tomatoes, lemon juice and the shallot and boil the mixture until the liquid is reduced to about 2 tablespoons.

Reduce the heat to moderately low and whisk in the butter, 1 bit at a time, lifting the skillet from the heat occasionally to let the mixture cool, adding each new bit before the previous one has melted completely. The sauce should not get hot enough to liquefy. It should be the consistency of thin hollandaise.

Divide the salmon among 6 heated plates and serve it with the sauce.

*You can chop the tomatoes and the shallot in the food processor, especially if you are making more than one recipe for a larger crowd.)

5

SALADS

Smoked Salmon Salad
by Leslie Cerier, Amherst, MA

A beautiful meal for entertaining: rolled pieces of smoked salmon on top of a dill potato and string bean salad.

Dairy-free, wheat-free, corn-free

Serves 4

> *1 pound baby new potatoes, 20 little potatoes (3 cups)*
> *1/2 pound string beans, sliced (2 cups)*
> *1/2 pound smoked salmon, sugar-free*

Dressing:
> *1 small bunch of dill, 3/4 cup with stems removed*
> *1/3 cup soy mayonnaise*
> *Optional: 1/4 teaspoon pepper or to taste*

Scrub and boil potatoes in water to cover till tender, about 12 to 15 minutes. Drain and cut potatoes into bite-sized pieces. Put potatoes and string beans into a mixing bowl.

To make the dressing, blend the mayonnaise, dill, and pepper in a food processor. Taste and adjust the flavor, if desired. Stir the dressing into the vegetable mixture and transfer the salad to a serving platter.

Remove the smoked salmon from the package. Cut the slices in half lengthwise. Roll up each piece of smoked salmon and arrange on the string bean potato mixture in a circular design. Serve.

Pasta Salad with Goat Cheese
by Ann Starbare, Crystal Brook Farm, Sterling, MA

This salad is easy to prepare and a delight to eat, perfect for a busy summer day.

Vegetarian, corn-free

Serves 6–8

1 pound dried rotelli or similar pasta
6 tablespoons extra-virgin olive oil
2 tablespoons cider vinegar
2 cups orange or red cherry tomato, halved
1 cup coarsely chopped fresh basil
8 ounces chevre (goat cheese)
1 teaspoon salt
1 teaspoon black pepper
Optional: 3–5 whole basil leaves

Cook pasta according to package instructions until al dente. Drain into a colander. Transfer pasta into a large serving bowl and add the olive oil, vinegar, tomatoes and basil. Crumble the goat cheese over the top and toss all the ingredients together, adding the salt and pepper to taste. Garnish with whole basil leaves. Serve the salad warm or at room temperature.

Baked Goat Cheese Salad
by Ann Starbare, Crystal Brook Farm, Sterling, MA

This light summer dish fills the niche for lunch and dinner, casual or elegant dining.

Vegetarian, corn-free

Serves 8

1/4 cup extra-virgin olive oil
1 cup plain bread crumbs, preferably homemade
8 ounces chevre, sliced into 8 1/2-inch-thick pieces
1/2 pound mixed salad greens
1 teaspoon red wine vinegar
pinch of salt, to taste
1 pint cherry tomatoes, stemmed and halved
2 bell peppers, preferably yellow and red, julienne

Heat 1 tablespoon of the olive oil in a small pan over medium heat. Add the bread crumbs and stir, cooking until golden brown, about 5 minutes.

Preheat oven to 500 degrees. Place the goat cheese pieces in the pan with bread crumbs, one at a time, and coat evenly on all sides. Press the crumbs gently into the cheese. Place pieces on a baking sheet lined with aluminum foil. Bake for 5 minutes. Meanwhile, combine the greens with remaining olive oil, vinegar and salt. Toss well.

To serve, divide the greens on individual dinner plates. Arrange 4 or 5 pepper strips cleverly in the center. Place the rounds of baked chevre on top. Decorate around the greens with tomatoes wedges.

Salade Nicoise
by Evan DuVerlie, Shutesbury, MA

Here's a French-influenced dish we eat for lunch on many summer days.

Wheat-free, dairy-free, corn-free

Serves 4

> 4–5 medium potatoes
> 1/2 pound green beans
> 1/3 cup red wine vinegar
> 1/3–1/2 cup olive oil
> 1/4 cup fresh basil, chopped
> sea salt to taste
> ground black pepper to taste
> 2–3 ripe tomatoes
> 1 can tuna, drained
> 4 hard-cooked eggs, cooled and peeled
> 1 green pepper
> 1/2 medium red onion
> 1 cup black olives
> 2 tablespoons capers

Boil the potatoes and green beans (separately, or one after the other) until tender when poked by a fork. Drain, cool and cut into bite-sized pieces.

Mix oil, vinegar, basil, salt and pepper in the bottom of a large bowl. Add potatoes and beans and stir gently. Cut the rest of the ingredients into bite-sized pieces and add to potatoes. Stir gently. If possible, let the salad marinate for an hour so the flavors can set. Serve at room temperature.

Spinach and Shiitake Mushroom Salad
with Creamy Herb Yogurt Dressing
by D. B. Dawson, Newark Natural Foods Co-op, Newark, DE

Quick and simple to make, this salad has a delightful zing from cranberries and lemon, and goes well with my Tomato Spinach Soup on page 80. If you like, you may prepare the dressing ahead of time.

Vegetarian, wheat-free, corn-free

Serves 8

> *about 2 pounds of spinach*
> *2 cups sliced shiitake mushrooms*

Dressing:
> *1 cup low-fat yogurt*
> *1 tablespoon extra-virgin olive oil*
> *1/4 cup fresh basil, chopped*
> *2 tablespoons fresh parsley, chopped*
> *2 tablespoons fresh cilantro, chopped*
> *2 tablespoons fresh chives, chopped*
> *2 tablespoons fresh lemon juice*
> *1/2 teaspoon salt*
> *1/4 teaspoon black pepper*
> *1 shallot, minced*
> *2 cloves garlic, minced*

Garnish:
> *1/2 cup rehydrated cranberries*
> *1/2 cup toasted walnuts*

Toss spinach and mushrooms into a large mixing bowl. Mix all the dressing ingredients in a separate bowl. Keep dressing on the side or pour it over the salad. Garnish with cranberries and walnuts.

Warm Spinach and Orange Salad
by Rebecca Broida Gart, Delicious Magazine, Denver, CO

The appealing flavors of oranges, walnuts and spinach make this a wonderful salad.

Vegetarian, wheat-free, corn-free

Serves 6–8

> 1 pound baby spinach, washed, stems removed
> 2 large naval oranges
> 1/3 cup unsalted walnuts
> 1/4 cup red wine vinegar
> 1 tablespoon walnut oil
> salt and pepper
> 1/4 cup gorgonzola

Rip spinach and place in a vegetable steamer on the stove, with a small amount of water. Steam lightly for about 30 seconds, until spinach is warm but not completely wilted.

With a sharp knife, peel orange and divide orange into segments. Transfer to a large bowl. Add spinach.

Blend walnut oil, vinegar, salt and pepper and spoon mixture over the orange and spinach in the bowl. Toast walnuts and sprinkle over salad. Add salt and pepper to taste. Crumble gorgonzola and sprinkle over salad. Serve immediately.

Five Element Salad
by Marie Summerwood, Syracuse, NY

This salad contains all five tastes: sweet, sour, bitter, spicy and salty.

Vegan, wheat-free, corn-free, heart smart, low fat

Serves 6–8

> 1 10- to 12-inch wakame sea vegetable
> 1 cup red cabbage

4 tablespoons umeboshi vinegar
3/4 teaspoon roasted sesame oil
1 cup grated carrot
1 cup grated daikon radish
chopped parsley or scallions for garnish

Soak wakame in warm water for 20 minutes. Discard water and cut wakame into small pieces. Set aside.

Chop cabbage thinly, as for coleslaw, and cook in the umeboshi vinegar until nearly cooked, 6 to 8 minutes. Drain and cool, then mix in the sesame oil.

This is a composed salad. Arrange all the vegetables attractively on a platter or in a shallow bowl. Garnish and serve.

Cucumber-Alaria Salad

by Larch Hanson, Maine Seaweed Company, Steuben, ME

Alaria is a versatile sea vegetable harvested off the coast of Maine and is a wonderful substitute for Japanese wakame in soup, bean and vegetable dishes, and in this tasty salad.

Vegan, wheat-free, corn-free, heart smart, low fat

Serves 2–4

1 pound cucumbers (2–3), thinly sliced
1 teaspoon sea salt
1 18-inch strip of alaria, cut dry with a scissors into 1/4-inch slices
2 tablespoons lemon juice
1/2 tablespoon sesame oil
1 teaspoon rice vinegar
1/2–1 red pepper, diced

Put sliced cucumbers in a mixing bowl and sprinkle with salt. Set aside for thirty minutes. Soak pieces of alaria in water for 15 minutes.

Combine lemon juice, sesame oil, and rice vinegar in a small separate bowl.

Lightly rinse cucumbers. Rinse and squeeze out extra water from alaria. Combine all the vegetables and toss with the dressing.

Arame Salad

by Mindy Goldis, World Peace Kitchen, San Diego, CA

Sea vegetable salads are tasty and mineral rich. Arame has the texture of angel hair pasta with a sweet briny Asian flavor.

Vegan, wheat-free, corn-free, heart smart, low fat

Serves 4

> *1 cup dry arame*
> *2 medium carrots, cut into matchsticks*
> *3–4 scallions/green onions, cut in thin diagonals*
> *1/2 purple cabbage, shredded*
> *20–30 snow peas/sugar peas, cut in thin diagonals*
> *1/4–1/2 cup dulse flakes*
> *tahini sesame butter—to thicken the salad—start with 1–2 tablespoons (add more as needed)*
> *1 lemon, juiced (add more according to taste)*
> *2–3 tablespoons umeboshi vinegar*
> *1–2 tablespoons sesame oil*

Soak arame in water to cover for 5 to 7 minutes, or cook arame for 10 to 20 minutes. Combine all ingredients with arame. Add seasonings. Taste and adjust seasonings, if desired.

Quinoa Tabouli Salad

by Mindy Goldis, World Peace Kitchen, San Diego, CA

Quinoa (pronounced keen-wa) originally comes from the Andes mountains of South America. It is high in protein and has all essential amino acids. Quinoa is also light, tasty, quick to prepare and easy to digest.

Vegan, wheat-free, corn-free, heart smart, low fat

Serves 4

> *1 cup quinoa, rinsed*
> *2 cups water*
> *pinch of sea salt*

1 small bunch parsley, chopped (1 cup)
1/2 cup chopped scallions
2 tablespoon fresh mint
1 clove garlic, minced
whole lettuce leaves
1/2 teaspoon fresh basil
1 lemon or 1/2 cup lemon juice
1/4 cup olive oil
1/4 cup sliced olives
sea salt to taste—use small amount
umeboshi vinegar, to taste

Place quinoa in a strainer and rinse well under running water. Set aside to drain. Bring water to a boil in a 1 quart stock or sauce pot. Add quinoa and pinch of sea salt. Simmer for 15 minutes or until the water is absorbed.

Place all the ingredients except the lettuce leaves and olives in a mixing bowl, and toss together lightly. Adjust seasonings, if desired. Chill for 1 hour or more to allow flavor to blend.

Wash and dry lettuce leaves and use them to line a large salad bowl. Add seasoned quinoa. Garnish with olives.

Fruited Chicken Salad
by Janelle Scheidecker, Meadow Farm Foods, Fergus Falls, MN

Chicken and fruit paired with a flavorful curry dressing is "mmm." This main course salad makes a great side dish and appetizer, too. If you want to make the chicken and dressing a few hours ahead of time, add the fruit prior to serving.

Wheat-free, corn-free, heart smart

Serves 4

Dressing:
3/4 cup plain yogurt
1 teaspoon lime zest
1 teaspoon curry powder
1 teaspoon ground ginger

Salad:

1/2 cup seasoned rice vinegar
1 bay leaf
2 chicken breasts, boneless, skinless
1 cup chopped celery
2 naval oranges, peeled and segmented
1 apple (your choice), chopped
1 banana, peeled and sliced
1 cup raisins
1 cup sliced almonds
6–8 cups assorted greens—tear into bite-sized pieces (mesclun mix or spring mix)

Combine dressing ingredients, mixing well. Place in a covered container and refrigerate while preparing salad.

Heat rice vinegar in medium saucepan. Add bay leaf and chicken breasts. Simmer over low heat for 20 minutes or until chicken is no longer pink in the center. Remove chicken and chop into bite-sized pieces. Let cool (can be refrigerated).

While chicken is cooling, chop celery, prepare oranges, apple and banana, and place them in a large bowl. Stir in raisins, almonds and cooled chicken. Add dressing and mix gently.

To serve, place about 2 cups of assorted greens on each of 4 plates. Top with the chicken salad by dividing evenly over the greens on each plate.

6

DRESSINGS,
CHUTNEYS,
SAUCES
AND RELISHES

Spiced Tomato and Peach Relish
by Nava Atlas, Hudson Valley, NY

Serve this piquant relish with Indian-style curries like a chutney.

Vegan, wheat-free, corn-free

Makes about 2 cups

> *1 tablespoon light vegetable oil*
> *1 medium onion, finely chopped*
> *1 tablespoon honey or pure maple syrup*
> *1 pound very ripe, juicy tomatoes, diced*
> *2–3 sweet peaches, pitted and diced*
> *1/4 cup raisins or currants*
> *1 teaspoon grated fresh ginger, or more to taste*
> *1 teaspoon ground cumin*
> *1/2 teaspoon ground cinnamon*
> *Optional: 1/4 teaspoon cayenne or red pepper flakes, or to taste*

Heat the oil in a large saucepan. Add the onion and sauté until translucent. Add the remaining ingredients and bring to a simmer. Cook over low heat, covered, for 10 to 15 minutes, stirring occasionally. The tomatoes and peaches should be tender but not overdone. Taste to correct seasonings, then simmer over very low heat for another 5 minutes, uncovered. Allow to cool to room temperature and serve.

Sea Veggie Caesar Dressing
by Denise Roseland, Lakewinds Natural Foods, Minnetonka, MN

Serve this delicious dressing with chopped romaine lettuce, croutons, strips of nori, or grated parmesan cheese.

Vegan, wheat-free, corn-free

Serves 8

> *1 tablespoon minced garlic*
> *2 teaspoons Dijon mustard*
> *2 teaspoons umebushi plum paste*
> *3 tablespoons balsamic vinegar*

3 tablespoons lemon juice
1 tablespoon white miso
6 ounces soft silken tofu
1/3 cup canola oil
1/3 cup olive oil
1/2 teaspoon chopped dulse

Combine garlic, mustard, umebushi paste, balsamic vinegar, lemon juice, white miso and tofu in food processor. Process until creamy. With the machine running, add canola and olive oils in a thin stream, blending until fully incorporated.

Zesty Onion Dressing
by Kemper Carlsen, Shutesbury, MA

Here is a special salad dressing that is well balanced and satisfying.

Vegan, wheat-free, corn-free, low fat

Makes 1 pint

1 cup olive oil (can reduce this by more than 1/2 by replacing with 1/8 cup flax seeds and 1/2 cup water blended well)
1/4 cup cider vinegar
1/4 cup tamari
1/2 onion, sliced (vidalia onions are my preference)
1/8 cup nutritional yeast

Blend all ingredients till creamy in a blender.

Tofu Garlic Dressing
by Olivia Tacelli, Arlington, MA

Here is a creamy, garlicky sauce that is great on salad, steamed veggies, rice, or pasta. Sauce keeps for 7 days in the refrigerator.

Vegan, wheat-free, corn-free

Makes about 3 1/2 cups

1 pound tofu, any firmness, drained
1 cup parsley greens (no stems)
2 tablespoons chopped garlic
4 teaspoons dried oregano
1 tablespoon chili powder
1 teaspoon black pepper
1/2 cup olive oil
1/2 cup tamari
1/2 cup water, or more
(test for salt)

Blend all ingredients in a blender till smooth. Adjust water for consistency.

Ziji's Tomato-Ginger Dressing
by Beth Goren, Shutesbury, MA

For that special party, here's a zesty treat.

Vegan, wheat-free, corn-free

Makes 1 pint

1/4 cup tamari
1/4 cup oil
1/2 cup tomato puree
2 tablespoons cider vinegar
1 teaspoon garlic powder
1 teaspoon ginger powder
1/4 medium onion, about 1/4 cup
2 tablespoons maple syrup or to taste

Blend all the ingredients in a blender or food processor. Taste and adjust the seasonings, if desired.

Cilantro-Coconut Chutney
by Olivia Tacelli, Arlington, MA

Try a dollop of this pesto-like condiment in soup or any dish with curry.

Vegan, wheat-free, corn-free

Makes about 2 cups

> *2 cups cilantro, greens and stems, minced or processed in food processor*
> *1 cup mint leaves, minced or processed in food processor*
> *1 small onion, minced (1/4 cup)*
> *4 cloves garlic, minced*
> *1 inch ginger, peeled and minced*
> *1/2 cup coconut*
> *1/2 cup walnuts*
> *3 tablespoons rice syrup*
> *1 or 2 jalapenos, minced (depending on how hot you like it)*
> *1 1/2 teaspoons salt*
> *2 tablespoons safflower oil*
> *Optional: a bit of water*

Blend all ingredients in a food processor, blender or bowl. Use water, if needed, to make the consistency smooth.

Hot Sauce
by Evan DuVerlie, Shutesbury, MA

We make a batch of this simple hot sauce every two weeks. I put it on just about everything from eggs to soup to tomato juice.

Vegan, wheat-free, corn-free, heart smart, low fat

Makes a little over a quart

> *28-ounce can of ground, peeled or diced tomatoes*
> *1 medium clove garlic*

3/4 cup wine vinegar
1–2 tablespoons crushed red pepper or about 6 whole dried hot chilies*
2 teaspoons salt

*You may want to start out with 1 tablespoon hot pepper, and add more, if desired. Keep in mind that the hotness mellows and flavors meld after a short time in the bottle in the refrigerator.

Combine all ingredients in a blender until the peppers and garlic are fairly well pulverized. (It's okay if there are still some visible bits of pepper seeds in the mix.) Taste and adjust the seasonings, if desired. Serve or pour the sauce into jars, and refrigerate.

Rosemary and Basil Tomato Sauce
by Mary Carolyn Sullivan, Brazos Natural Foods, Bryan, TX

Fresh rosemary makes this aromatic and nutrient-rich sauce for pasta extra special and unique.

Vegan, wheat-free, corn-free, heart smart, low fat

Serves 4

1/8 cup extra-virgin olive oil
1 whole bulb of garlic, chopped
1 red onion, chopped
3 tablespoons fresh rosemary
10 Roma tomatoes, sliced
2 cups mushrooms, sliced
1/2 cup fresh basil, chopped
2 tablespoons ground black pepper

In a large saucepan, add oil, garlic, rosemary and onion. Sauté till onions are translucent, about 5 minutes. Add tomatoes, mushrooms, basil and pepper. Cover and simmer for 30 minutes, stirring occasionally. Taste and adjust the seasonings, if desired.

Pavarotti Sauce

by Deedy Marble, Culinary Educator, Sterling, MA

I ALWAYS double or triple this recipe. It freezes well; that is, if there is any left over. Serve over pasta, ravioli or rice.

Vegan, wheat-free, corn-free, heart smart, low fat

Makes almost 1 quart

> *1 teaspoon crushed garlic*
> *3/4 cup water*
> *2 teaspoons best quality olive oil*
> *2 medium red bell peppers, seeded and thinly sliced*
> *1/2 cup diced carrot*
> *1 medium onion, thinly sliced and separated into rings*
> *1 1/2 cup crushed tomatoes*
> *1 Bartlett pear, pared, cored and diced*
> *1 teaspoon crushed fennel seeds*

In a saucepan, heat the olive oil over medium heat. Add peppers, carrot and onion. Sauté 6 to 7 minutes or until vegetables are soft. Add remaining ingredients. Bring to a boil. Cover and simmer for 40 minutes, stirring occasionally.

Mushroom Gravy

by Sharon K. Reimer, Country Cupboard Natural Foods, Russelville, AR

Here is a vegetarian brown gravy that is wonderful on potatoes or veggie burgers.

Vegan option, corn-free, heart smart, low fat

Serves 4–6

> *1/4 cup canola oil or butter*
> *2–4 tablespoons tamari*
> *1/2 cup sliced mushrooms*
> *pinch of chili pepper flakes*

1/4 cup whole wheat flour
2–3 tablespoons nutritional yeast flakes
2 cups water

Sauté the mushrooms in oil and tamari for 5 minutes. Stir in flour and nutritional yeast. Gradually add water—stirring continually to avoid lumps. Cook on low until bubbly and thickened. Pour hot over mashed potatoes or burgers.

BBQ Marinade
by Dongmee K. Smith, Four Chimneys Farm Winery, Himrod, NY

You can use this as a glaze or marinade for grilled meat, tempeh, tofu and fish. It keeps really well and does not need to be refrigerated! Recipe can be halved or quartered. Keeps for months!

Vegetarian, wheat-free, corn-free

Makes about 4 cups

1 quart red or white grape juice
1 cup soy sauce or tamari
3 cloves garlic, chopped
4 tablespoons butter

Put juice and tamari in a saucepan; bring to a boil, then reduce heat to a simmer for 3 minutes. Add garlic and butter until the liquid thickens enough to cover the back of the spoon, about 20 minutes. Remove from heat and let it cool.

Cider Glaze
by Tagan Engel, Brooklyn, NY

This is delicious on tofu, fish, chicken, stir-fries, roasted or steamed vegetables, toast and even ice cream.

Vegan, wheat-free, corn-free, heart smart, fat-free

Makes 1 1/2 cups

1 gallon apple cider
2 star anise
1 teaspoon whole black peppercorns
2 slices fresh ginger
2 cloves
3 cinnamon sticks
1/4 teaspoon cider vinegar or lemon juice
pinch salt

Place first six ingredients (cider through cinnamon stick) into a large stock pot. Bring cider to a boil and then lower heat so that cider stays at a low boil. Reduce cider down to 1 cup, approximately 1 hour. When syrup is nearing desired thickness, add 1/4 teaspoon vinegar or lemon juice, and a pinch of salt to taste. Remove spices with a slotted spoon or by pouring the syrup through a sieve.

Depending on the pectin content of your cider, the syrup will vary in thickness; you can add water a teaspoon at a time to thin syrup, or continue reducing to thicken. Syrup will thicken naturally when cool. Keeps for 1 month in the refrigerator.

Serving suggestions
Tofu: Marinate tofu for 20 minutes in syrup. Bake at 400 degrees, turning once till light brown on both sides.

Vegetables: Roast root vegetables such as carrots, yams, parsnips, and onions by tossing with olive oil to coat, season with salt and pepper, and roast on cookie sheets at 450 degrees, till brown on edges, 20 to 30 minutes. Let vegetables cool till warm, not hot. Toss with a few tablespoons of cider syrup and fresh baby salad greens, and you have an elegant delicious meal.

Chicken and fish: Use as a marinade, glaze or sauce.

7

SOUPS

Potato Leek Soup
by Leslie Cerier, Amherst, MA

Simple and creamy, this vegan soup is low fat and flavorful.

Vegan, wheat-free, corn-free, heart smart, low fat

> *1 tablespoon extra-virgin olive oil*
> *2 large leeks, rinsed and sliced, (white part + 3 inches of green—3 cups)*
> *2 cloves garlic, peeled and sliced*
> *2 large potatoes, sliced (3 1/2 cups)*
> *1 1/4 cups water*
> *2 3/4 cups soy milk*
> *1 teaspoon dried thyme, or tarragon or dill*
> *Season to taste with tamari or salt and pepper*

Place oil in a large stock pot. Sauté garlic and leeks for 2 minutes. Add potatoes, and sauté for 5 minutes. Add water and soy milk. Bring to a boil, cover and simmer for 20 minutes, or till potatoes are soft. Puree the soup in small batches in a blender or food processor. Add thyme or other herbs, plus tamari or salt and pepper to taste.

Curried Vegetable Soup
by Leslie Cerier, Amherst, MA

Light and satisfying, this soup is perfect for a warm spring day.

Vegan, wheat-free, corn-free, heart smart, fat-free

Serves 6–8

> *1 cup red lentils, rinsed*
> *10 cups of water*
> *1 strip of dulse*
> *Optional: 1 tablespoon dried nettles*
> *1 large onion, sliced (1 1/2 cups)*
> *1 large sweet potato or yam, sliced (4 cups)*

1 small cauliflower, sliced (2 cups)
1 tablespoon + 1 teaspoon curry powder
2 teaspoons garam masala
1 bunch chopped cilantro or 1 teaspoon cardamom or dried coriander
2 teaspoon sea salt or to taste

Boil and simmer red lentils, dulse, nettles and water for 15 minutes. Add onions, yam, and cauliflower. Simmer 15 to 20 minutes till vegetables are tender or as soft as you like them. Add spices and salt. Taste and adjust the seasoning, if desired.

Leek, Potato and Carrot Pottage (or "Soupe de Meme")
by Evan Du Verlie, Leverett, MA

My grandmother in France would make this for lunch nearly every day. It's simple, delicious and nutritious.

Vegetarian, wheat-free, corn-free

Serves 4–6

2 quarts water
2 medium leeks, white parts, and some of the green
6 medium potatoes (Yukon Gold or Yellow Finns are our favorites), rinsed
3 medium carrots
Salt and fresh ground pepper
Olive oil to drizzle
Optional: shredded Swiss-type cheese for topping

Start heating water in a large pot. Meanwhile, slice leeks into 1/4-inch slices, and make sure to wash well. Chop carrots and potatoes into medium-sized chunks; peeling is not necessary. Add vegetables to the water, adding more water if necessary to cover. Simmer 1/2 hour, until soft.

Puree soup with a hand blender. (If you are using a regular blender, carefully scoop out cooked vegetables and blend. Only fill blender halfway to avoid overflow!) Add salt and pepper to taste. Drizzle with olive oil and top with a bit of shredded cheese.

7 6

Cream of Spring Greens Soup
by Nava Atlas, Hudson Valley, NY

If your fridge is bursting with seasonal greens, here's a great way to use them. Make sure all greens are very well washed!

Vegetarian, wheat-free, corn-free, heart smart, fat-free

Serves 6–8

1 1/2 tablespoons light olive oil
1 large onion, chopped
2 to 3 cloves garlic, minced
2 large potatoes, peeled and diced
2 small or 1 large vegetable bouillon cube
2 bunches Asian greens, any variety, thick mid-ribs trimmed, leaves coarsely chopped
1 good-sized bunch spinach (6 to 8 ounces), stemmed
2 heads green lettuce, coarsely chopped
1/2 to 1 cup parsley leaves
1 cup low-fat milk or soy milk, or as needed
salt and freshly ground pepper to taste
Optional garnish—one or more: Low-fat sour cream, low-fat plain yogurt or soy yogurt

Heat the oil in a soup pot. Add the onion and sauté until translucent. Add the garlic and continue to sauté until the onion is golden. Add the potatoes and bouillon cube with 3 cups water, or enough to cover. Bring to a simmer, then simmer gently, covered, until the potato is tender, about 15 to 20 minutes. Add the Asian greens and simmer, covered, for 5 minutes. Add the spinach leaves and cover; cook just until they wilt down. Add the lettuce leaves and parsley and simmer over low heat for 5 minutes, or until all the greens are just tender.

Puree the mixture in batches until smooth in a food processor or blender. Return to the soup pot and stir in 1 cup of milk or soy milk, or as needed for a slightly thick consistency. Season with salt and pepper and serve.

For an optional but very pretty garnish, combine a little sour cream and milk in a small milk pitcher or spouted measuring cup, mix well, using enough milk to make a pourable consistency. Slowly pour a spiral design over the top of each serving of soup.

Roasted Yellow Pepper and Corn Milk Gazpacho
by Tagan Engle, Brooklyn, NY

Make this soup when corn is fresh and in season. And for those of you that like it hot, add a jalapeno pepper to spice it up.

Vegan, wheat-free, heart smart, low fat

Serves 4

3 yellow bell peppers
6 ears of corn
3 cups water
4 cucumbers
1 clove garlic, sliced
1 small red onion, finely diced
Optional: 1 jalapeno pepper for a little spicy kick
1/3 cup lemon juice
2 tablespoons olive oil
salt to taste
2 tablespoons chopped chives for garnish
garnish with yogurt

To roast peppers: place whole peppers directly onto a gas burner and char each side, rotating the peppers until all the skin is black. Immediately place the peppers into a container and cover tightly either with a lid or plastic wrap for 15 to 20 minutes. (This will steam the peppers and help to release the skin from the flesh without losing all their flavor to the water in a conventional ice bath). Uncover peppers. Peel skins off with your fingers, and pull out seeds and stem. Have a bowl of water on hand to rinse your fingers and rinse as much of the blackened skin off as possible. Finely dice one pepper and set aside for garnish. Reserve other peppers for gazpacho base.

Cut the kernels off of all the ears of corn by standing the ear on it's end and slicing down the sides. Blanch 1 cup of corn kernels in boiling water for 60 seconds, until lightly cooked and still firm; set aside with peppers for garnish. Place half of the raw corn in a food processor or blender and add 1 1/2 cups water. Puree until the corn is very fine, and the liquid is milky. Pour the puree through a fine sieve and squeeze out all the liquid from the chopped corn. This is the "broth, or corn milk," for your soup. Repeat with the other half of the raw corn.

Peel and seed the cucumbers. Chop them into large pieces and set aside. Place garlic clove, 1/2 of onion, jalapeno pepper, 1/3 of the cucumber pieces and 2 teaspoons of salt in the bowl of a food processor. Puree until very fine, adding a bit of corn milk as needed to help ingredients blend. Add the remaining cucumber and peppers to the mixture in the food processor and puree. Empty the puree into a large bowl.

Place the remaining onion, blanched corn, and reserved diced peppers into the food processor with 1 cup of corn milk. Pulse 5 times to lightly chop ingredients. Add this into the large bowl, stir in lemon juice and remaining corn milk. Season with salt to taste. You may thin the soup with a bit of water if desired.

Chill; then serve with a spoonful of yogurt and a sprinkle of chives on each bowl.

Creamy Spinach Tofu Soup
by Ziporah Hildebrandt, www.ravensridge.bookworks.com, Shutesbury, MA

Simply omit the onion, and you've got a super-quick meal.

Vegan, wheat-free, corn-free, heart smart, low fat

Serves 4

> *2 medium onions*
> *2 teaspoons olive oil*
> *2 teaspoons tamari*
> *8 cups washed, stemmed fresh spinach*
> *1 pound tofu*
> *2 medium garlic clove (optional)*
> *6 cups water*

In saucepan, sauté onion in olive oil over medium heat till translucent. Stir in tamari. Add spinach, lower heat and cover. Add a little water if necessary. When spinach is just wilted, still bright deep green, put the onion and spinach into a blender or food processor with the tofu and garlic. Blend until smooth using enough water to process.

Heat remainder of water. Add the blended ingredients, stir and heat. Do not boil. Season to taste, serve. Enjoy.

Winter Squash Kelp Soup
by Wendy Karush, Wendy's Good Food, Hancock, ME

Heart healthy seaweeds make this fall and winter soup yummy.

Vegan, wheat-free, corn-free, heart smart,

Serves 4

> 1 5- to 6-inch piece of kelp
> 5 cups water
> 1 medium onion, chopped
> 1 medium winter squash, cubed (about 1 quart)
> 4 tablespoons parsley, chopped
> 2 drops toasted sesame oil
> 1–2 tablespoons miso or to taste
> 2 cups cooked chick peas

Simmer kelp and water for 20 to 30 minutes in a covered soup pot. Remove kelp and cut into small pieces. Return kelp to pot, add onion and squash. (Add more water if necessary or desired). Cover and simmer until squash is soft, 20 to 30 minutes, or pressure cook 5 to 10 minutes. Stir in parsley, toasted sesame oil, miso and chick peas. Heat gently for 5 minutes and serve.

Shiitake Tastebud Soup
by Olivia Tacelli, Arlington, MA

Colorful and full of many textures, this soup has an array of satisfying tastes.

Vegetarian option, wheat-free, heart smart, low fat

Serves about 10

> 2 quarts stock (veggie/beef, homemade or bouillon)
> 2 to 3 inches of ginger root, peeled and cut into match sticks
> 2 cups sliced shiitake mushroom caps (stems removed)
> 3 tablespoons sesame, safflower or mild-tasting olive oil
> 1 yellow onion, sliced in moons (about 1 cup packed)
> 1/2 red bell pepper, sliced into 1- or 2-inch strips (about 3/4 cup)
> 1 carrot, cut into match sticks

1/2 can baby corn, sliced on the diagonal into 1/2-inch pieces (about 3/4 cup)
chili peppers, dried (crumbled) or fresh (minced), as many as you like, start with
one and see
3/4 cup tamari or soy sauce
1/4 cup apple cider or brown rice vinegar
1/4 cup honey
1 teaspoon salt
1/2 pound firm tofu, cut into tiny cubes
1 cup packed thinly sliced greens (bok choy, Swiss chard, spinach)
3 tablespoons toasted sesame oil
3 tablespoons cornstarch
1/3 cup cold water
2 scallions, sliced into thin rings

Add ginger peels and mushroom stems to the stock and simmer while you prep the other ingredients.

Sauté onion, ginger, pepper and mushrooms in oil for 10 minutes over medium-high heat in a large stock pot. Add carrot, baby corn, chili pepper, and sauté 3 more minutes.

Strain stock and add to vegetables with tamari, vinegar, honey, and salt. Simmer over medium heat till very hot. Taste and adjust to balance hot, sour, salty and sweet flavors. Add tofu, greens and toasted sesame oil. Simmer 5 minutes.

In a separate bowl, mix cold water and cornstarch. Stir into soup till it dissolves and thickens soup and gives it a glossy sheen within minutes. Add scallion. Enjoy!

Tomato Spinach Soup
by Denise Roseland, Lakewinds Natural Foods, Minnetonka, MN

This delicious soup is quick to prepare, very warming, and has a nifty flavor that goes well with my Spinach and Shiitake Mushroom Salad on page 57.

Vegetarian, corn-free

Serves 4–6

1 tablespoon olive oil
1 cup diced onion
1 teaspoon dried basil
1 teaspoon dried thyme

1 cup sliced mushrooms
32-ounce can of crushed tomatoes
3 cups chopped spinach
3 tablespoons flour
3 cups vegetable broth
1/2 teaspoon salt
1/2 teaspoon black pepper

Heat oil in a stock pot. Add onions, basil, thyme and mushrooms. Sauté till tender, about 5 minutes. Stir in tomatoes and spinach. Simmer 10 minutes. Whisk flour and broth together. Add to tomatoes in several additions. Season to taste with salt and pepper. Simmer until thickened slightly. Serve.

Variation:
For a creamier soup, substitute 1 cup of half and half for 1 cup of broth.

Lentil Fresh Herb Soup
by D. B. Dawson, Newark Natural Foods Co-op, Newark, DE

Everyone will love this soup. If there is any left over, add a little water and you will find that it tastes even better the next day. Serve with some fresh whole grain bread for a complete meal.

Vegan, wheat-free, corn-free, heart smart, low fat

Serves 4–6

2 tablespoons olive oil
2 cups onions, chopped
2 celery stalks, chopped
2 medium carrots, chopped
6 cloves garlic, chopped
1 bay leaf
1/2 cup white wine
6 cups water
1 pound dry lentils
3 tomatoes, chopped
1/4 cup fresh basil, chopped
2 tablespoons fresh thyme, chopped
2 tablespoons fresh oregano, chopped
2 tablespoons fresh sage, chopped

2 tablespoons fresh flat-leaf parsley, chopped
1 teaspoon salt
1/2 teaspoon black pepper

Heat oil over medium-high heat. Add and sauté onions, celery and carrots until onions are translucent. Add garlic and sauté for 2 minutes or so; add bay leaf. Stir in wine and reduce it down by about half. Add vegetable stock and lentils. Bring to a boil, reduce heat; cover and simmer gently for thirty minutes or until the lentils are soft. Add tomatoes and fresh herbs. Simmer for a moment or two. Add salt and pepper. Taste and adjust seasonings, if desired.

Cream of Mushroom Soup
by Marie Summerwood, Syracuse, NY

Blend cashews with water to make your own cashew cream. Add sautéed mushrooms for this quick and easy soup.

Vegan, wheat-free, corn-free

Serves 4–5

1 cup raw cashews
4 1/2 cups water
2 tablespoons Greek olive oil
1 large onion, diced
4 cups mushrooms, sliced
1 teaspoon sea salt
2 tablespoons tamari or to taste
chopped watercress/scallions for garnish

Blend cashews and 2 cups water until totally creamy in a blender or food processor. The cashews will blend into a thick cream with no mash left.

Heat oil in a heavy skillet and sauté onions until translucent. Add mushrooms and sauté on medium until they become juicy. Add 2 1/2 cups water and salt. Boil and simmer covered 15 minutes or until the mushrooms are cooked. Remove from heat. Stir in cashew cream and tamari. Return to a very low flame and heat to serving temperature. Do not boil or the cream will begin to separate. Garnish and serve immediately.

Sweet Fish Chowder
by Leslie Cerier, Amherst, MA

As the vegetables soften, the broth becomes sweeter. A spinach salad and buttered whole-wheat baguette is all you need to round out this meal.

Wheat-free, corn-free, heart smart, low fat

Serves 4–6

>   *6 cups water*
>   *2 bay leaves*
>   *2 delicata squashes, peeled, seeded and sliced into bite-sized pieces (4–5 cups)*
>   *1 onion, sliced (1 cup)*
>   *2 stalks celery, sliced (1 cup)*
>   *4 small red potatoes, sliced (2 cups)*
>   *1/4 teaspoon nutmeg*
>   *1/4 teaspoon black pepper*
>   *1 teaspoon sea salt*
>   *1 1/2 pounds scrod, cusk, or monkfish, or an assortment*
>   *Optional: garnish soup with chopped parsley, chives or scallions*

Boil and simmer vegetables and bay leaves 45 minutes to an hour. The vegetables soften and the broth becomes sweeter with longer simmering. Lightly rinse fish and add it whole to the soup. Simmer 2 to 3 minutes and add nutmeg, sea salt and pepper. Simmer 10 minutes, or until fish naturally falls apart into chunky, white, bite-sized pieces. Taste and adjust the seasonings, adding more salt and pepper if you like. Serve garnished or plain.

Granny's Chicken Soup
by Leslie Cerier, Amherst, MA

Nourishing chicken and vegetable soup warm us on a cold day like a hug from grandma. For a hearty meal, you can add cooked noodles or rice. Serve each bowl garnished with fresh chopped herbs for a beautiful dinner.

Wheat-free, corn-free

Serves 6–8

1 whole chicken
4 quarts water
2 teaspoons sea salt
1 large onion or leek, chunky cut (1–2 cups)
1 carrot, "roll" or chunky cut (1 cup)
1 small celeriac, peeled and cut into 1/2-inch pieces (1–2 cups)
1 parsnip, sliced (1 cup)
1 turnip, sliced (1 cup)
Optional: garnish with 1 bunch parsley or dill, chopped

Remove as much fat and skin from the chicken as possible. Rinse the chicken. Put it in a large stock pot with water and sea salt. Add the vegetables. (If necessary, add enough water to barely cover the chicken. The wings and drum sticks will rise above the water.) Bring the pot to a boil, reduce heat to a simmer and cover. Turn the chicken over with tongs several times to ensure even cooking. When the meat falls off the bones easily as you turn the chicken (after about 90 minutes or more), turn off the heat. Remove all skin, discard the bones, and break the chicken into bite-sized pieces. Serve garnished with parsley or dill, if desired.

Note: to reduce fat, refrigerate the soup overnight, then skim fat from the top surface.

Chilled Cucumber Soup
by Deedy Marble, Culinary Educator, Sterling, MA

How great is it to make a tasty soup in a matter of minutes?

Vegetarian option, wheat-free, corn-free

Makes about 5 cups

1 quart buttermilk
2 large young cucumbers, peeled, seeded and coarsely chopped
1 tablespoon vinegar
1 tablespoon chopped fresh dill
3 scallions, chopped (white and light green parts)
2 tablespoon fresh chives
1 tablespoon Dijon mustard

1/2 teaspoon herb salt, or to taste
freshly ground pepper
garnish with dill, chopped chives, pimentos, or edible flowers such as chive
blossoms
Optional: add cooked shrimp

Put 2 cups of the buttermilk into a blender or food processor and all the remaining ingredients. Blend until as smooth as you like, and transfer to a large bowl or jar. Add the remaining 2 cups buttermilk. Stir well. Chill thoroughly. Serve garnished with bits of pimiento, chopped chives or dill. I especially like edible flowers. Chive blossoms are lovely floating on this soup. You may also add pieces of cooked shrimp.

Caribbean Ginger Carrot Soup
by Ruth Hampton, Oneota Community Food Co-op, Decorah, IA

A delicate soup for all seasons. The ginger is warming in the winter, yet it's light enough for a hot summer day. The color alone will cheer you up! Serve with red beans and rice for a fantastic Caribbean dinner.

Vegan, wheat-free, corn-free, low fat

Serves 4

4 cups carrots, coarsely chopped
1/2 cup onion, chopped
1/2 cup apple, chopped
2 cups water or vegetable stock
1/2 cup cashews
1 tablespoon fresh ginger
1/2 teaspoon cumin, toasted and ground
dash of salt
dash of pepper
1/2 teaspoon lemon juice
2 cups rice milk

Simmer all ingredients, except rice milk and lemon, until carrots are tender. Puree carrot mixture in a blender or food processor. Add the lemon and rice milk, and adjust seasonings, if desired.

Energy Soup

by Jesse Schwartz, President, Living Tree Community Foods,
www.livingtreecommunity.com, Berkeley CA

I call this an energy soup because in my experience it is easily digested and
has the effects of enhancing one's aliveness and well being. We've been
preparing "energy soup" at Living Tree Community for over a decade. We
serve it at every meal. Here is the basic recipe.

Raw, vegan, wheat-free, corn-free, heart smart, low fat

Serves 1

> *3 carrots, sliced thinly or diced*
> *2 beets, sliced thinly or diced*
> *1 apple or cucumber (in season), diced*
> *chopped parsley, celery, kale, collards, arugula, endive, spinach, cabbage,*
> *cilantro, chard and lettuce (your choice)*
> *avocado*
> *lemon juice*
> *spring water or carrot juice*

Put the mixture into blender. Add spring water or freshly made carrot juice.
If you want to supercharge the drink, add a handful of wheat grass. Blend
into a thick, smooth soup. Serve immediately.

Variations:
1. Grind in a seed mill or coffee grinder some flax, sesame, sunflower,
   pumpkin or chia seeds and toss it in.
2. Add a chopped apple.

8

SIDE DISHES

Maple Cornbread
by Erin Wheeler, Upper Valley Food Cooperative, White River Junction, VT

Spelt flour gives this cornbread a delicious nutty flavor. It is moist and delicious like grandma used to bake.

Vegan, low fat

Makes 1 loaf

> *1 3/4 cups spelt flour*
> *2/3 cup cornmeal*
> *1 tablespoon baking powder*
> *1/2 teaspoon sea salt*
> *1/3 cup maple syrup*
> *3/4 cup soy milk*
> *1/2 cup canola oil*

Preheat oven to 400 degrees. Combine and mix all the ingredients in a large mixing bowl. Pour into oiled 9-inch round pan and bake for 20 minutes.

Chick Peas with Tomatoes and Ginger
by Leslie Cerier, Amherst, MA

Vegan, wheat-free, corn-free, heart smart, low fat

Serves 4–6

> *1 tablespoon extra-virgin olive oil*
> *2 inches of ginger, grated (2 tablespoons)*
> *1 onion, sliced (1 cup)*
> *4 cups chopped plum tomatoes*
> *2 cups cooked chick peas*
> *1/4 teaspoon turmeric*
> *1 teaspoon cumin*
> *1 teaspoon cinnamon*
> *1/2 teaspoon sea salt, or to taste*
> *1/4 teaspoon pepper, or to taste*
> *1 bunch cilantro, chopped*

Sauté onions, ginger, and tomatoes in oil till tomatoes are juicy, about 10 minutes. Add chick peas, and spices. Stir and simmer for 5 to 10 minutes to blend flavors. Season to taste with salt and pepper. Garnish with cilantro.

Stuffed Artichokes
by Mary Ellen Salvini, Amherst, MA

Here is a favorite side dish I serve my family for the holidays. When I make a big antipasto, this side dish will serve 10, and if you make a smaller meal, figure one artichoke per person, and this recipe will serve 5.

Vegetarian, corn-free

Serves 5–10

> *4 jumbo artichokes or 5–6 large ones*
> *6 cloves garlic, minced*
> *l large onion, minced*
> *3 tablespoons + 1/3 cup olive oil*
> *1 1/2 cups bread crumbs made from stale whole wheat bread, grated*
> *1/4 cup parmesan or mixture of romano and parmesan cheese*
> *2 large eggs, beaten*
> *Optional: 1 tablespoon milk*
> *2 tablespoons raisins*
> *2 tablespoons pine nuts*
> *1 1/2 cups water*
> *1/3 cup lemon juice*
> *4 cloves garlic, smashed and set aside*
> *Optional: 1/2 teaspoon dried hot pepper, if you like, or black pepper to taste*
> *1/2 cup chopped fresh parsley, pressed down*
> *salt to taste*

Square off the tips of the artichoke leaves, and remove inner prickly part of each artichoke, leaving the heart. Chop off stem and set aside. Cover with cold salted water for 15 minutes and then drain.

Peel and chop stems of artichokes and sauté with onion in 3 tablespoons of olive oil till onions are transparent, caramelizing them for 5 to 10 minutes. When they are soft, add 2 cloves minced garlic and cook a little more. Remove from heat and cool.

Add bread crumbs, cheese, eggs, salt and pepper to taste, chopped parsley, raisins and pine nuts. If crumbs do not stick together, you can add a tablespoon of milk. Fill each artichoke with mixture and place in large deep skillet or pot that will hold them. Add water, the 1/3 cup olive oil, lemon juice, 4 smashed garlic cloves, and hot pepper or black pepper and salt, if you like. Cover and simmer about 30 minutes and then turn each over and continue simmering, checking every 10 minutes and turning.* Should be done in 55 to 60 minutes. Taste a leaf for doneness.

*You can use a large roasting pan and cover with foil as a substitute for a large skillet and use 2 burners on stove top to cook.

Curried Cauliflower, Potatoes and Chick Peas
by Laura Sylvester, Shutesbury, MA

Perfect for the busy chef, this dish is quick, easy and delicious. Serve with a green vegetable and hearty bread for a satisfying meal.

Vegan, wheat-free, corn-free, heart smart, low fat

Serves four as a main course or six as a side dish

> *4 large Yukon Gold potatoes*
> *1 head cauliflower, sliced into florets*
> *1 1/2 tablespoons olive oil*
> *1 large onion, sliced*
> *5 cloves garlic, sliced*
> *1/2 teaspoon salt, or to taste*
> *1/2 teaspoon cayenne pepper*
> *1/2 teaspoon cumin*
> *1/2 teaspoon turmeric*
> *1/2 teaspoon curry powder*
> *1 14-ounce can chick peas (garbanzo beans) (or use 2 cups cooked chick peas)*

Scrub potatoes and cut into 3-inch chunks. Bring to boil in medium-sized pot. Cook 10 to 12 minutes until just tender.

Chop onion and sauté five minutes in olive oil. Add cauliflower, garlic, salt, cayenne pepper, cumin, turmeric, and curry powder. Drain potatoes and chick peas and add to cauliflower mixture. Stir gently and continue to cook for 5 to 10 more minutes. Taste and adjust the seasonings.

Black Beans with Ginger and Mustard Greens
by Leslie Cerier, Amherst, MA

This creamy ginger-flavored bean stew is a potent side dish or accompaniment to steamed rice. It is also great to dip bread in. Ginger, a traditional spice in Indian, African and Oriental cooking, adds a wonderful pungent quality to bean dishes. If desired, use two cups cooked or canned black beans and omit step one. Drain and set aside.

Vegan, wheat-free, corn-free, heart smart, low fat

Serves 4–6

> 1 cup dried black beans, soaked overnight in cold water to cover
> 1 1-inch piece of ginger, sliced very thin
> 1 small bunch mustard greens, sliced (3 cups)
> 1 tablespoon Dijon or other prepared mustard
> 3 tablespoons sorghum or molasses
> 1 tablespoon tamari

Rinse beans thoroughly and put them in a pot with several cups of water. Cook until the beans are tender, about 1 1/2 hours. Drain and set aside.

Bring ginger and 1/2 cup water to boil in a medium pot. Simmer for 5 minutes. Add beans and simmer for 5 minutes. Stir in mustard greens and simmer until tender, for 3 to 5 minutes. Add molasses, mustard and tamari. Stir in additional water if desired to thin consistency. Serve immediately or at room temperature.

Kale with Soy Garlic Butter
by Olivia Tacelli, Arlington, MA

Here is a savory and addictive side dish. You can also serve this delicious garlic sauce on green beans, broccoli, zucchini, baked or boiled potatoes, sautéed tofu, rice and pasta. It will last 2 weeks in your fridge so feel free to make extra to have around.

Vegetarian, wheat-free, corn-free

Serves 8

Sauce:

> *1 stick butter or 1/2 cup olive oil*
> *2 tablespoons minced garlic*
> *1/3 cup tamari*
> *1/2 lemon, squeezed*
> *1 tablespoon nutritional yeast*
> *1 teaspoon paprika*
> *2 bunches kale, washed and cut into strips*

Melt butter in saucepan. Add garlic and simmer over medium heat for 5 minutes. Add tamari, lemon juice, yeast and paprika. Simmer 5 minutes. Remove from heat and set aside.

Put 2 inches of water in a soup pot with a steamer basket at the bottom. Add kale and cover. Put over high heat. Once water is boiling, steam kale for 8 minutes. Transfer kale with tongs to a serving bowl. Drizzle 1/2 cup butter sauce over kale (you may have some left over) and toss quickly. Serve.

Dulse and Kale

by Larch Hanson, Maine Seaweed Company, Steuben, ME

Dulse is a tasty sea vegetable, very high in iron, and delicious as a snack. You can add dulse to a salad like spinach, simmer it, or sauté it as I did here.

Vegan, wheat-free, corn-free, heart smart, low fat

Serves 4

> *2 tablespoons oil*
> *2 cloves garlic, minced*
> *2 quarts chopped kale*
> *1/2 cup dulse, soaked, drained, and chopped*
> *1/3 cup roasted sunflower seeds*

Sauté garlic in oil for 2 minutes. Add kale and sauté until the color deepens. Add dulse and roasted sunflower seeds. Cover and steam about 2 minutes.

Italian Greens
by Len Huber, Shutesbury, MA

Quick, easy and very tasty, you can make this versatile dish with a variety of greens as well as red or green cabbage.

Vegan, wheat-free, corn-free, heart smart, low fat

Serves 2–4

> *1 bunch of greens such as kale, spinach, or collards, rinsed (about 6 cups)*
> *(You can also use red or green cabbage.)*
> *2–3 tablespoons extra-virgin olive oil*
> *1 teaspoon garlic powder*
> *1/2 teaspoon sea salt*
> *1/4 teaspoon pepper*

Place greens in a steamer and steam them till not quite tender, about 3 minutes. Chop greens into bite-sized pieces. In a large skillet, add olive oil and greens, garlic powder, salt and pepper. Sauté for 5 to 10 minutes till greens are as tender as you like. Season to taste.

Mediterranean Spinach
by Sylvia Brallier, Las Vegas, NV

Spinach cooked with olives, nuts and mushrooms is fantastic served over pasta.

Vegetarian, wheat-free, corn-free

Serves 4

> *3 tablespoons olive oil*
> *1/2 cup walnuts, almonds, or pecans, coarsely chopped*
> *3–6 cloves of garlic, minced*

6 ounces mushrooms, cleaned and sliced
16 ounces fresh-washed spinach
1/2 cup kalamata olives, seeded and sliced
1/3 cup fresh basil leaves, coarsely chopped
1/4 pound feta cheese, crumbled
tamari or salt, to taste

Sauté nuts, garlic and mushrooms in olive oil on medium heat until cooked, about 5 minutes. Add olives, spinach, basil and 1/8 cup water. Cover and steam spinach until thoroughly wilted, but still light green.
Stir up the vegetables. Top with crumbled feta. Cover again for a minute or so to melt the cheese, then add the tamari or salt, and mix it all together.

Gingered Tofu
by Marie Summerwood, Syracuse, NY

Serve over rice for a tasty meal.

Vegetarian, wheat-free, corn-free

Serves 4–6

1 pound firm tofu
1 1/2 cups water
6 tablespoons tamari
2 tablespoons soft butter
6 inches fresh ginger root, peeled

Slice or cube the tofu and set aside. Slice the ginger root into thin wheels to shorten the fibers. Put ginger in a blender with tamari, water and butter. Pour over tofu and marinate the tofu in the ginger butter sauce for at least an hour in a baking dish.
    Broil tofu for about 15 to 20 minutes or until the tofu begins to turn brown. If you like, you can turn the tofu over and broil the other side for 15 to 20 minutes.

Winter Vegetables
by Marie Summerwood, Syracuse, NY

This hearty, comforting vegetable stew is easy to prepare.

Vegan, wheat-free, corn-free, heart smart, low fat

Serves 4

> *1 12- to 14-inch piece of dried wakame*
> *2 tablespoons olive oil*
> *1 large burdock root (14 inches), scrubbed and sliced thin*
> *4 turnips, sliced into 1/2-inch rounds*
> *2 medium carrots, sliced into 1/2-inch rounds*
> *1 large onion, sliced*
> *2 teaspoons dill seed*
> *2 cups water*
> *2 tablespoons kudzu or 4 tablespoons arrowroot*
> *3 tablespoons tamari or to taste*
> *garnish with chopped parsley*

Soak wakame in cold water for 10 minutes or until soft. Drain, chop, set aside.

Heat oil in a heavy skillet and sauté onions over medium heat until translucent. Add burdock root and sauté about 15 minutes on slightly lower heat, until the earthy aroma mellows. Stir in carrots, turnips and dill seeds. Add 1 cup water and wakame; cover and simmer about 15 minutes.

Dissolve kudzu in the rest of the water; add to the vegetables with the tamari. Stir until it begins to boil and thicken. Garnish and serve.

The Healthy Habit Veggie Burger
by Jennifer Matey, The Healthy Habit, Milford, NJ

Portabello mushrooms, rice and nuts make a tasty vegan burger. Seasoned with chili powder, it is anything but bland.

Vegan, corn-free

Serves 6–8

2 pounds portabella mushrooms, chopped
4 cups cooked brown rice
8 cups bread crumbs
4 cups chopped carrots (or carrot pulp from juicing)
1 cup toasted nuts (any kind except peanuts)
2 medium onions, chopped
6 cloves garlic, chopped (or 1 tablespoon granulated garlic)
1 tablespoon salt
1 teaspoon pepper
2–4 tablespoons chili powder

Preheat the oven to 300 degrees. Mix mushrooms, rice, nuts, carrots, onions, bread crumbs and garlic in a large bowl. Grind up mixture in batches in the food processor. Add salt, pepper and chili powder. Mix well. Shape into patties sealing edges well. Place on cookie sheet. Bake for 20 minutes. Flip over burgers and bake for 15 minutes.

Baked Yams with Maple Lime Glaze
by Denise Roseland, Lakewinds Natural Foods, Minnetonka, MN

Wonderful!

Vegan, corn-free, heart smart, low fat

Serves 8

1/2 cup lime juice
1/2 cup water
1/2 cup maple syrup
3 medium yams, peeled and thinly sliced
salt
2 large red onions, thinly sliced
zest of 1 lime
1 cup bread crumbs
1 teaspoon dried sage
1/2 teaspoon black pepper

Preheat oven to 350 degrees. Place 2 tablespoons lime juice in a small saucepan. Set aside. Place remaining lime juice in another saucepan. Stir in water and 1 tablespoon maple syrup. Bring to a boil, lower heat and continue to cook until reduced to 1/2 cup, about 10 to 15 minutes.

Spray or lightly oil a 13-inch × 9-inch baking pan. Arrange one third of yam slices in a layer in the baking dish. Sprinkle with salt. Top with half of the onions. Season again with salt. Arrange another layer of yams, another layer of onions and finish with the remaining yams.

Add the lime zest to the reduced glaze and pour evenly over yam mixture. Scatter bread crumbs evenly over the top, cover and bake for 30 minutes. Uncover and bake for an additional 45 minutes or until crumbs are golden and yams are tender. Remove from oven and let sit 10 minutes before serving. Meanwhile, heat remaining lime juice with the remaining maple syrup, sage and pepper just until warm. To serve, scoop yams onto individual plates and drizzle with warm lime-maple mixture.

Pasta Italian Style
by Leslie Cerier, Amherst, MA

A delightful pasta dish seasoned with sun-dried tomatoes marinated in white wine and fresh basil. This dish is quick and easy if you marinate the tomatoes earlier in the day.

Vegan, corn-free, low fat

Serves 4–6

> *5 cups cooked pasta*
> *2/3 cup white wine*
> *1 cup sun-dried tomatoes, not packed in oil*
> *3 tablespoons olive oil*
> *2 onions, sliced (2 cups)*
> *10 cloves of garlic, sliced*
> *2 zucchinis, sliced (2 cups)*
> *2 bunches of fresh basil (1 1/2 cup leaves)*
> *2 tablespoons umeboshi vinegar or lemon juice and sea salt to taste*

Marinate sun-dried tomatoes in wine for 2 hours.

In a heavy skillet or wok, sauté the onions and garlic in 1 tablespoon of olive oil for 2 minutes. Add marinated tomatoes and wine. Sauté/simmer for 5 minutes. Add zucchini and sauté for 5 minutes. Stir in basil and umeboshi vinegar. Turn off heat and drizzle on 2 tablespoons of olive oil. Stir and taste. Adjust the seasonings, if desired.

Thai Peanut Stir Fry

by Vanessa Paulman, Amherst, MA

Here I used a wild mushroom, called hen of the woods, also known as maitake, but you can use other wild or domestic mushrooms such as waxy caps, white button, portobello, crimini, and oyster mushrooms in this delicious Thai peanut stir fry.

Vegan, corn-free

Serves 4–6

1 tablespoon sesame oil
1 tablespoon fresh ginger, diced or shredded
1 bulb garlic, cloves peeled and diced
1 small onion, diced
1 teaspoon spicy sesame oil or cayenne
1 pound mushrooms, sliced (hen of the woods or a mixture of domestic and wild mushrooms: waxy caps, white button, portobello, crimini or oyster)
1 green pepper, chopped
2 cups cauliflower, chopped small
1 cup red cabbage, chopped small
1 cup bok choy, chopped
3 tablespoons "crunchy" peanut butter
2 tablespoons tamari
1 tablespoon tahini
1/2–1 cup water
8-ounce package soba (buckwheat noodles) cooked

Sauté onions, garlic and ginger in sesame oil in a wok until tender, about 5 minutes. Add and stir fry spicy sesame oil, vegetables and mushrooms, 5 to 10 minutes, till mushrooms cook down and cauliflower is as tender as you like. Turn off the heat.

In a large mixing bowl, whisk peanut butter, tamari, tahini, and 1/2 cup water until smooth. Add the other 1/2 cup of water if necessary to make a smooth sauce. Pour onto stir fry. Toss with cooked buckwheat noodles.

Paradise Rice

by Carol Joyce, White Buffalo Herbs, Warwick, MA

Close your eyes, take a bite of this creamy rice with a hint of spice, and you will feel the sultry breezes of the Caribbean.

Vegan, wheat-free, corn-free

Serves 4

1/8 cup dried small red peas (available in Caribbean stores, or substitute another dried bean like kidney beans, or omit beans)
14 ounces coconut milk
7 ounces + 1 tablespoon water
1 cup brown rice
2 garlic cloves crushed
1/2 Scotch Bonnet (habanera pepper) cut into tiny strips
pinch freshly grated nutmeg (can use powder, instead)
Optional: pinch sea salt, pinch white pepper

Soak red peas in water overnight, then drain and rinse before using, or try this quick soak method: bring beans and 2 cups water to a boil, take off the stove and let soak for 1 hour.

Bring coconut milk and water to a boil in a heavy saucepan. Add rice and bring back to a boil. Lower heat to a simmer. Add garlic, red peas, Scotch Bonnet and nutmeg. Cover pan and simmer for 45 minutes. Serve piping hot as a side dish. Terrific with pork, lamb or veggies.

Italian Style Vegetable Stew

by Leslie Cerier, Amherst, MA

I love this stew as a side dish or topping for pizza or pasta. Try it garnished with crumbled feta or grated parmesan.

Vegan, wheat-free, corn-free

Serves 4–6

1 medium-large eggplant (6 cups), sliced into bite-sized chunks (cut 1/2-inch rounds and then slice into 4–6 bite-sized pieces)
juice of 1 lemon (1/3 cup)
2 teaspoons sea salt
4 dried morel mushrooms
10 sun-dried tomatoes, cut into smaller pieces with a scissors
1 large onion, sliced (1 1/2 cups)
8 cloves garlic, peeled and whole
1 large carrot, sliced (1 cup)
5 tablespoons extra-virgin olive oil
2 tablespoons fresh basil or 2 teaspoons dried
1 sprig rosemary (1 teaspoon fresh leaves or 1/3 teaspoon dry)
2 heaping tablespoons fresh oregano leaves or 2 teaspoons dry

Preheat the oven to 400 degrees. Cut the eggplant and put it into a bowl with 1 teaspoon sea salt and the lemon juice. Let it marinate at least 30 minutes while you slice the other vegetables.

Drain and discard the excess liquid from the eggplant. Put the eggplant and all the other ingredients into a large mixing bowl, including the other teaspoon of sea salt. Mix well and transfer to a baking dish or crock. Make sure that the dried mushrooms and tomatoes are covered by the other vegetables. Cover and bake for 45 minutes. Taste the vegetables to see if they are as tender as you like them, and adjust the seasonings, if desired.

9

DESSERTS

Sesame Bars
by Kemper Carlsen, Shutesbury, MA

Salt-free, wheat-free and that's not all. These taste like decadent shortbread cookies.

Vegetarian, wheat-free, corn-free

Makes 1 1/2 dozen cookies

> *1/2 cup lightly toasted, unhulled sesame seeds*
> *1/3 cup canola oil*
> *6 tablespoons honey (the honey is important for keeping the bars together—don't substitute)*
> *1 tablespoon Egg Replacer or 1 1/2 tablespoons flax seeds mixed with 1/2 cup water—spoon out the 1 tablespoon from this.*
> *1 cup oat flour (or make your own—blend 1 cup oats in a blender)*
> *1/2 cup brown rice flour*
> *1/2 teaspoon vanilla*

Preheat oven to 350 degrees. Toast the sesame seeds gently on a dry skillet until slightly brown. Mix all the ingredients together and pat into a cookie sheet with edges. Make the dough 1/8 to 1/4 inch thick. Bake for 12 to 20 minutes; take out when edges start to turn light brown. Cut by pressing large knife into pan making sections before cookies cool.

Best Chocolate Chip Mint Cookies
by Michelle Huber, Shutesbury, MA

Delicious chocolate chip cookies with a touch of mint, my fav!

Vegan, corn-free

Makes about 3 dozen cookies

> *3 1/8 cups whole wheat pastry flour*
> *1/4 teaspoon sea salt*
> *1 teaspoon vanilla*

3/4 teaspoon mint extract
1/2 cup canola oil + 1 teaspoon for the cookie sheet
2/3 cup maple syrup
1 cup chocolate chips

Preheat oven to 375 degrees. Combine and mix together all the ingredients except 1 teaspoon canola oil. Lightly oil a cookie sheet with 1 teaspoon of oil. Using your hands, shape the dough into walnut-sized balls and place them onto the cookie sheet about 1/2 inch apart. Bake for 10 minutes. Let them cool for about 10 minutes before handling and eating.

Chocolate Chocolate Chip Cookies
by Leslie Cerier, Amherst, MA

Teff's high calcium and iron profile lead me to believe, for better or worse, that these delicious cookies are a healthy indulgence. Teff's naturally dark color and subtle chocolatelike flavor adds to the fun! (An 8-ounce serving of teff is equal to the 32% of the USDA for calcium and 80% for iron.)

Vegan, wheat-free, corn-free

Makes 12–18 depending on how big you shape the cookies

2 1/2 cups teff flour
1/2 cup cocoa powder
1 tablespoon arrowroot
1 tablespoon baking powder
1/2 teaspoon sea salt
1 teaspoon vanilla
2/3 cup canola oil
2/3 cup maple syrup
2/3 cup chocolate chips

Preheat oven to 375 degrees. Combine and mix together all the ingredients. Using your hands, shape the dough into round patties about 1/2 inch thick and 2–3 inches round. Bake for 10 minutes. When these come out of the oven, they may appear soft; do not be fooled into thinking they need more baking. As they cool, they become crisper.

Nutty Cookies
by Len Huber, Shutesbury, MA

Kids of all ages will love these cookies. The nuts and nut extracts give these cookies a delicious, rich, almost buttery flavor.

Vegan, corn-free

Makes 2–3 dozen cookies

> *2 cups whole wheat pastry flour*
> *1/3 cup maple syrup*
> *1/3 cup + 1 teaspoon canola oil*
> *1/4 teaspoon sea salt*
> *1 cup chopped walnuts*
> *2 tablespoons vanilla*
> *1/2 teaspoon hazelnut extract*

Preheat the oven to 350 degrees. Combine and mix all of the ingredients except 1 teaspoon of oil in a large mixing bowl. Lightly oil a cookie sheet with 1 teaspoon oil. Take a tablespoon of cookie dough and place it onto cookie sheet, gently pressing batter down with a the back of the spoon or your hand, making 2-inch round cookies. Bake them for 15 minutes. Let them cool for about 10 minutes before transferring to a cooling rack or platter.

Magic Maple Butter Cookies
by Susan Modelski, Parkade Health Shoppe, Manchester, CT

Here's one that the kids will love, or share them with your special sweetheart or friends.

Vegetarian, corn-free

Makes 30 cookies

> *1 cup whole wheat flour*
> *1/2 cup sweet or salted butter (1 stick)*
> *1/2 cup maple syrup*
> *1 egg*

1 teaspoon vanilla extract
Optional: 1 cup finely chopped walnuts

Begin with all the ingredients at room temperature. Put flour and butter in a mixing bowl and mix them together. Add and mix in maple syrup. In a separate bowl, scramble egg and add it to the flour mixture. Add vanilla, then add walnuts. Mix thoroughly, cover and chill in refrigerator for an hour or two.

Preheat the oven to 375 degrees. Spoon dough with a teaspoon onto a greased baking sheet (I use a nonstick cooking spray that's a blend of organic canola and olive oil), shaping cookies with your hands if you want a rounder cookie. Bake 12 to 15 minutes or till edges brown. Let cool slightly, just a minute or two, before transferring to racks or plates to finish cooling.

Magic Chocolate Cake
by Kemper Carlsen, Shutesbury, MA

This cake is magic because it is mixed and baked in one pan!

Vegetarian, corn-free

Serves 8–10

1 1/2 cups organic whole wheat pastry flour
1/2 teaspoon salt
1 teaspoon baking soda
5 tablespoons cocoa powder (or 4 tablespoons carob powder)
3/4 cup honey
1 teaspoon vanilla
1 tablespoon cider or white vinegar
3/4 cup cold water
1/3 cup oil
Optional: 1/4 cup chocolate chips

Preheat oven to 350. Sift all dry ingredients twice into a 9-inch pie pan. Make two depressions in the flour mix. In one pour vanilla and oil, in the other pour the vinegar. Pour the water over it all and stir till well blended. Be sure to get all along the edges. Right before baking you can chose to sprinkle 1/4 cup vegan chocolate chips over the top. Do not mix in as the chips will burn to the bottom of the pan. Bake for 25 to 30 minutes.

Carob Fudge Brownies

by Dongmee K. Smith, Four Chimneys Farm Winery, Himrod, NY

For extra flavor, you may roast the carob powder before you bake with it. To roast carob: spread out the powder on a cookie sheet (no oil on it) and bake in 325 degree oven for 20 to 25 minutes.

Vegan

Serves 6–8

Flax seed emulsion:
> *2 teaspoons flax seeds*
> *2 tablespoons water*

Wet Ingredients:
> *3/4 cup corn oil*
> *3/4 cup rice syrup*
> *2 teaspoons vanilla*
> *1/2 cup water*
> *3/4 cup chopped dates*

Dry Ingredients:
> *3/4 cup carob powder*
> *1 1/2 cup whole wheat pastry flour*
> *1/4 teaspoon sea salt*
> *2 teaspoons baking powder*
> *3/4 cup chopped nuts*

Preheat the oven to 350 degrees. Put flax seeds and 2 tablespoons water in a small bowl for 5 to 10 minutes or so. Then add this to the food processor along with the other wet ingredients. Blend, until smooth. In a medium-sized bowl, mix the dry ingredients except the nuts. Add the wet mixture into the dry mixture until well blended. Add the nuts. Bake it in a well-greased baking dish (8 × 8 inches) for 40 to 45 minutes.

Raw Tahini Treats
by Katherine Tarr, The Herb Shop, Mt Pleasant, UT

This nutritious treat will satisfy your sweet tooth. Feel free to experiment and vary the recipe by adding wheat germ, lecithin, protein powder, popped amaranth, or nutritional yeast in place of some of the ground up nuts and seeds. I even made it once using powdered spirulina. I liked it, but everyone else thought it was weird because it was green.

Raw, vegetarian, dairy-free, wheat-free, corn-free

Makes 1 loaf

> *1 cup of honey*
> *1 cup raw tahini or raw almond butter*
> *2 cups ground raw nuts and seeds, (almonds, flax seeds, sesame seeds, sunflower seeds, etc.)*
> *1 teaspoon vanilla*
> *1 cup unsweetened coconut*
> *1 cup raisins or dates*
> *Optional: 1 cup grain-sweetened or date-sweetened carob chips, 1 cup additional chopped nuts*

Heat honey to melt, remove from heat. Add tahini or almond butter, and mix. Add the rest of the ingredients. Stir and knead. Press into a pie plate or loaf pan and cut in squares. Serve.

Refrigerate leftovers, if there are any.

Pecan Yummies
by Ziporah Hildebrandt, www.ravensridge.bookworks.com, Shutesbury, MA

Here is a high-protein, high-energy snack that is great with ice cream. You can make these really quickly by not measuring ingredients. Simply use equal amounts of honey and sunflower butter, then add rice flour until you get the proper texture. Results may be slightly different, but always good! Unlike cookies that contain eggs, butter and sugar, these don't spread, so ingredient proportions are not critical to success.

Vegetarian, wheat-free, corn-free

Makes 2 dozen cookies

> *1/2 cup sunflower butter*
> *1/2 cup honey*
> *pinch of salt*
> *3/4 cup rice flour*
> *2/3 cup pecan pieces*
> *2 tablespoons water*

Preheat oven to 325 degrees. Cream together sunflower butter, honey, and salt. Gradually add rice flour, if using a mixer. If beating by hand, add all at once and work in. Texture will be quite crumbly. Add pecan pieces and just enough water, about 2 tablespoons, to make a dough that will hold together. Flatten spoonfuls on a greased cookie sheet. Place close together as cookies will not spread. Bake in oven until beginning to brown at edges, about 10 to 12 minutes.

Variation: You could also make these with peanut butter and peanuts.

Date Nut Treats
by Michelle Huber, Shutesbury, MA

Kids love to make and eat these.

Vegetarian, raw, wheat-free, corn-free, heart smart, low fat

Makes 15 walnut-sized balls

> *1 cup tightly packed pitted dates*
> *4 tablespoons water*
> *1/4 teaspoon cardamom, or to taste*
> *1/2 teaspoon cinnamon, or to taste*
> *1/2 cup chopped walnuts*
> *3 tablespoons honey*
> *1/3 cup almonds, ground*

Put the dates in a food processor with the water, cardamom and cinnamon. Taste and adjust the seasonings, adding more spices, if desired. Pour the date mixture into a small mixing bowl.

Grind walnuts in the food processor, or coarsely chop. Mix walnuts into the date mixture and shape into walnut-sized balls. Drizzle and coat each ball with honey.

Grind almonds into a meal in the food processor. Pour ground almonds onto a cutting board or plate. Roll date nut balls in almond meal and serve.

No Bake Peach Cake
by Leslie Cerier, Amherst, MA

Quick and easy to make, this fat-free dessert is perfect for a snack or dessert on a hot summer's day.

Vegan, corn-free, heart smart, fat-free

Serves 6–8

> *4 cups organic peach juice*
> *2–3 cups sliced peaches (2 cups)*
> *pinch of sea salt*
> *1 3/4 cups cous cous*
> *1 teaspoon vanilla*
> *Optional: garnish with fresh edible flowers such as calendula or johnny jump-ups*

Bring the peaches, peach juice and salt to a boil. Add the cous cous and simmer for 3 minutes till the cous cous absorbs the juice. Turn off the heat. Stir in the vanilla. Transfer cous cous to an unoiled cake pan and let it cool to room temperature. Garnish with fresh edible flowers. Cut and serve.

As another option, you can also serve this for a breakfast cereal. It's quick and you don't have to wait for it to cool. Whatever you don't finish, you can pour into a cake pan and serve later for a snack or a dessert.

Fresh Lemon Pudding or Pie Filling
by Marie Summerwood, Syracuse, NY

Vegan, wheat-free, corn-free, heart smart, low fat

Serves 4–6

> *2/3 cup arrowroot or 1/2 cup kudzu*

1/2 cup fresh lemon juice
2 teaspoons agar agar powder
1 1/2 teaspoons grated fresh lemon rind
1/2 teaspoon sea salt
1 teaspoon vanilla extract
3 1/2 cups water
1 1/2 cups maple syrup

In a medium pot combine the arrowroot, agar agar and salt. Slowly add the water to dissolve the arrowroot and agar agar completely. Bring to a boil over medium heat, stirring often. Reduce the heat to low and simmer for 10 minutes, stirring often. Add everything else except the vanilla; mix well and simmer a few more minutes. Remove from heat and add the vanilla. Pour into bowl or baked pie shell and allow to set at room temperature. Serve at room temperature, or refrigerate if desired.

Baked Apples with Goat Cheese and Golden Raisins
by Ann Starbare, Crystal Brook Farm, Sterling, MA

Vegetarian, wheat-free, corn-free

Serves 6

6 baking apples, tart or mellow
10 ounces chevre
1/2 cup maple syrup
1/2 cup golden raisins
1/4 cup slivered almonds, toasted

Preheat oven to 375 degrees. Using a small paring knife, remove the core from each apple to within 1/2 inch of the bottom. Be careful not to cut all the way through to the bottom. Using a small spoon, scoop out a cavity in the center of the apple about 1 1/2 inches in diameter and 2 inches deep. Set aside.

In a small bowl, combine the goat cheese and maple syrup and use a hand held mixer to blend and mix them together until smooth. Add the raisins and stir to combine. Spoon the mixture into the hollowed-out apples, dividing it evenly and mounding it so that it barely rises above the tops. Sprinkle the almonds evenly over the filling.

Select a baking dish large enough to hold the apples snugly and line it with aluminum foil. Place the apples in the dish. Bake, uncovered, until the filling and almonds brown and the apples are very soft, as if about to collapse, about 45 minutes. Serve hot.

Coconut Rice Pudding
by Sylvia Brallier, Las Vegas, NV

Nourishing and easy to prepare, this pudding is festive and fun to eat.

Vegan, wheat-free, corn-free

Serves 4–6

> 1 cup brown rice
> 1/3 cup slivered almonds
> 2 teaspoons oil
> 1/3 cup shredded coconut
> 1 quart plain soy milk
> 1/3 cup maple syrup
> 1/2 teaspoon salt
> 1/2 teaspoon vanilla
> 1/2 teaspoon ground cardamom
> 1 ripe mango, cut into bite-sized chunks

Place the rice in a blender and reduce to a very course flour. Brown the slivered almonds in oil and set aside. Lightly brown the coconut in a frying pan and remove. Put the rice flour, soy milk, maple syrup, coconut, vanilla, cardamom and salt in a double boiler on medium heat. Stir occasionally. If the mixture becomes too thick, add a little more soy milk or water. Cook about 25 minutes. Serve the pudding warm garnished with the almonds and mango.

Coconut Rice with Fruit Pudding
by Sherrie Parke, Westside Natural Foods, Lahaina, HI

Aloha! Because coconuts are abundant on Maui, Hawaii, I like to drink the water for breakfast and make milk with the meat. For those of you on the mainland, please buy a can of coconut milk to make this delicious pudding.

Vegetarian with Vegan option, wheat-free, corn-free

Serves 6

> *1 cup basmati rice*
> *1 can lite coconut milk or 12 ounces fresh*
> *2–2 1/2 cups water (depends on how creamy you like)*
> *1 tablespoon coconut extract*
> *1/2 cup raisins*
> *1/8 cup sunflower seeds*
> *1 teaspoon safflower or sunflower oil*
> *Optional: 1 teaspoon ghee (omit if vegan)*
> *6 pitted dates, chopped*
> *1 tablespoon cinnamon*
> *1 tablespoon vanilla*
> *2 tablespoons honey or maple syrup*
> *1 tablespoon toasted, flaked coconut*

Soak the rice overnight. Rinse until water runs clear. Cook rice in coconut milk and 12–16 ounces of water, until rice is tender and there is a creamy sauce. Stir in coconut extract and turn off the heat. Set aside.

Boil raisins in 1/2 cup of water till plump. Set aside.

In a medium saucepan, toast sunflower seeds in oil and ghee. Add raisins with cooking water and dates. Simmer till dates are soft. Stir in cinnamon, vanilla, maple syrup. Turn off the heat. Put 1/4 inch of this mixture into individual serving cups. Top with 3/4 inch of the rice mixture. Sprinkle with toasted coconut and serve.

Apple Barley Pudding
by Becky Farris, Natural Health Organic Foods, Cape Girardeau, MO

This pudding is great topped with hot applesauce, hot soy milk or whipped cream.

Vegan, wheat-free, corn-free

Serves 4–6

> *3 peeled and diced Gala apples*
> *1/2 cup frozen apple juice concentrate*
> *2 teaspoons arrowroot powder*
> *1/2 teaspoon cinnamon*
> *2 tablespoons whole wheat pastry flour*

1 cup plain or unsweetened soy milk
2 cups cooked barley
1 teaspoon vanilla extract
1/3 cup date pieces
1/2 cup walnut pieces
1 tablespoon date sugar

Preheat oven to 400 degrees. Mix apples and apple juice concentrate together in a small saucepan over low heat. Simmer until apples are cooked, about 5 to 7 minutes. Remove from heat and stir in arrowroot powder and cinnamon.

Put pastry flour into a medium mixing bowl and slowly whisk in the soy milk. Blend in barley, vanilla, dates, walnuts and date sugar. Add and mix in apple mixture. Pour into a baking dish and bake covered for 45 minutes or until done in the center. Serve warm.

Pear Fig Crumb Pie
by Leslie Cerier, Amherst, MA

This pie is sweet indulgence and easy to make. Simply mix up the pie dough and press it into a pie pan. No need to refrigerate or roll. Using teff flour creates a slightly "chocolatey" flavored pie crust very high in calcium and iron. (An 8-ounce serving of teff is equal to the 32% of the USDA for calcium and 80% for iron.) Adding figs for the pie filling increases the amount of iron, too. Feel free to substitute your favorite seasonal fruits or pie fillings.

Vegan, wheat-free

Serves 8

Pie Crust:
2 cups teff flour
1/2 cup maple syrup
1/2 cup + 1 tablespoon corn oil or canola oil
1/2 teaspoon sea salt
1 tablespoon vanilla

Filling:
3 pears sliced thin
10 figs
pinch of sea salt

1/2 cup water
1 tablespoon kudzu or arrowroot

Preheat the oven to 375 degrees. Combine all the pie crust ingredients in a mixing bowl, leaving out 1 tablespoon canola oil for oiling the pie pan.

Lightly oil pie pan with 1 tablespoon canola oil and press 3/4 of the dough into it. (Reserve the rest of the dough for the crumb topping.) Poke holes with a fork. Bake it for 10 minutes.

While crust is baking, thinly slice pears and take the stems off the figs; place in a 2-quart saucepan with 1/4 cup water and a pinch of sea salt. Simmer for about 15 to 20 minutes or until the pears are tender.

Dissolve kudzu in 1/4 cup cold water. Stir it into the cooked pears. Then, pour filling into the baked pie crust. Crumble remaining teff dough on top. Bake for 10 minutes or until crumbs turn a slightly darker brown.

Ginger Pear Cake
by Leslie Cerier, Amherst, MA

Enjoy a slice of this cake with a dollop of sweet whipped tofu, whipped cream, ice cream or nondairy frozen dessert, and it is wonderful served on its own.

Vegan, corn-free option

Makes 2 loaves or 1 large cake

> *3 cups whole wheat pastry flour*
> *1/2 teaspoon sea salt*
> *2 tablespoons baking powder*
> *1 1/2 tablespoons ginger powder*
> *1 teaspoon cinnamon*
> *1 teaspoon nutmeg*
> *5 tablespoons flax seeds, ground*
> *1 pear, diced (1 cup)*
> *2 cups apple or pear juice*
> *1/2 cup + 1 tablespoon canola or corn oil*
> *3/4 cup maple syrup*
> *1 tablespoon vanilla*

Preheat oven to 350 degrees. No need to sift, just combine flour, salt, baking powder, ginger, cinnamon and nutmeg in a large mixing bowl. Grind flax seeds in a blender and add juice, 1/2 cup oil, vanilla and maple syrup. Blend briefly. Add and stir the wet ingredients into the dry ingredients. Lightly oil a 9-inch × 13-inch × 2-inch cake pan or two loaf pans with 1 tablespoon oil. Pour in cake batter. Bake for 40 minutes.

Happy Monkey Banana Pie
by Leslie Cerier, Amherst, MA

The banana date filling is so delicious and creamy that you could serve it as a pudding (without baking), if you like.

Vegetarian, dairy-free, wheat-free option, corn-free

Serves 6–8

Pie Crust:
> *2 cups whole wheat pastry flour, or barley flour, or a combination*
> *1/3 cup + 1 tablespoon canola oil*
> *1/3 cup maple syrup*
> *1/2 teaspoon sea salt*
> *Optional: 1 tablespoon vanilla*

Pie filling:
> *1 pound tofu, firm style*
> *1 1/8 cups pitted dates*
> *1 ripe banana*
> *1 tablespoon vanilla*
> *1/4 cup tahini*
> *2 tablespoons honey*

Preheat the oven to 375 degrees. Combine all the pie crust ingredients in a mixing bowl, leaving out 1 tablespoon canola oil for oiling the pie pan. If you decide to use barley flour, you may find that the dough is a little crumbly, and that is fine. Press dough into the pie pan. Poke holes with a fork. Bake it for 10 minutes. Add filling.

To prepare the filling, put all the ingredients in a food processor. Blend briefly, taste, and add more honey, if desired. Pour the filling into the pre-baked pie crust and bake for 10 minutes or until golden brown. Let it cool before serving.

Carrot Coconut Cake
by Leslie Cerier, Amherst, MA

Spelt flour has a nuttier flavor than wheat flour and makes delicious pastries like this carrot coconut cake.

Vegan, corn-free

Serves 6–8

> *2 cups spelt flour*
> *1/2 teaspoon sea salt*
> *1 tablespoon baking powder*
> *1/2 teaspoon cinnamon*
> *1/4 teaspoon cardamom*
> *1/4 teaspoon nutmeg*
> *1/4 cup shredded coconut*
> *1/4 cup walnuts*
> *1 cup grated carrots*
> *1/4 cup canola or corn oil + 1 teaspoon*
> *1/4 cup maple syrup*
> *1/2 cup rice milk or vanilla soy milk*
> *1/2 cup apple or pear juice*
> *1 1/2 teaspoons vanilla*

Preheat the oven to 350 degrees. In a large mixing bowl, combine the flour, baking powder, salt, cinnamon, nutmeg, cardamom, walnuts, coconut and grated carrots. Blend 1/4 cup oil, maple syrup, apple juice, rice milk and vanilla in a food processor or blender. Add and stir the wet and dry ingredients together till well blended. Lightly oil a 9-inch round cake pan or a loaf pan with 1 teaspoon of oil. Pour batter into cake pan. Bake for 35 minutes or until a toothpick inserted into the cake comes out dry.

Banana Cranberry Cake
by Leslie Cerier, Amherst, MA

This cake is a wonderful treat for dessert, breakfast or tea time.

Vegan, corn-free

Serves 6–8

> *3 cups whole wheat pastry flour*
> *1 tablespoon baking powder*
> *1/2 teaspoon sea salt*
> *1/4 teaspoon orange zest*
> *1/2 cup raisins*
> *1/2 cup walnuts*
> *1 cup fresh or frozen cranberries*
> *1 cup orange juice (fresh squeezed, if possible)*
> *2 bananas*
> *1 tablespoon vanilla*
> *1/2 cup canola oil + 1 tablespoon for oiling the cake pan*
> *1/2 cup maple syrup*

Preheat the oven to 375 degrees. Without sifting, combine the flour, baking powder, salt, zest, walnuts, raisins and cranberries in a large mixing bowl. Puree bananas in a blender with orange juice, vanilla, oil and maple syrup. Stir into mixing bowl. Oil cake pan with one tablespoon of oil. Pour batter into the cake pan. Bake for an hour. Stick a toothpick in the cake to check for doneness. If it is still wet, turn off the oven and let cake sit in the oven for about 10 minutes. Since there are so many cranberries, the cake may need just a little extra time to sit to dry out a little. Cool before serving.

Organic Foods Company Directory

Chino Valley Ranchers
Organic (also free-range) eggs
5611 Peck Road
Arcadia, CA 91006-5851
www.chinovalleyranchers.com
Email: David@chinovalleyranchers.com
Phone: 626-652-0890; 800-354-4503

Coombs Vermont Gourmet
Maple syrup
www.maplesource.com
Email: coombs@maplesource.com
Phone: 802-368-2513; 888-266-6271

Coonridge Organic Goat Cheese
Many flavors: natural; herbs and garlic;
roasted garlic; dried tomatoes, basil and
garlic; black peppercorn and herbs; herbes
de Provence; dillweed onion; habanero;
and more.
47 Coonridge Dairy
Pie Town, NM 87827
www.coonridge.com
Email: coonridge@starband.net
Phone: 1-888-410-8433 (voice mail)

Diamond Organics
Diamond Organics delivers overnight
nationwide a complete selection of fresh,
organically grown fruits, vegetables, brick-
oven baked breads, pastas, meats, dairy,
beer, wine, flowers, herbs, beans, grains and
a wide selection of prepared foods from
their own organic kitchen.
PO Box 2159
Freedom, CA 95019
Phone: 888-674-2642

Four Chimneys Farm Winery
Red, white, and fruit wines, grape juice,
vinegars and cooking wines
211 Hall Road
Himrod, NY 14842
www.fourchimneysorganicwines.com
Email: fourchim@htva.net

Phone: 607-243-7502
Distributed out of New York State by Almont
Wine Shop
104 Maple Avenue
Altamont, NY 12009
Phone: 877-NYS-WINE
Distributed out of NYS by Saratago Wine
Exchange
Phone: 518-580-9891
http://www.ny-wine.com

French Meadow Bakery
Yeast-free breads: hemp-sprouted bread,
spelt bread, woman's bread, men's bread,
health seed spelt bread, country baguette,
basil baguette, yeast-free bagels and pizza
crusts, and more.
2610 Lyndale Avenue South
Minneapolis, MN 55408
www.organicbread.com
Email: lrgordon@frenchmeadow.com
Phone: 877-No Yeast; 612-870-4740

Frey Vineyards Ltd.
Certified organic, Demeter Biodynamic,
family-owned winery, no sulfites added to
wines!
14000 Tomki Road
Tedwood Valley, CA 95470
www.freywine.com
Email: frey@pacific.net
Phone: 707-485-5177; 800-760-3739

Living Tree Community Foods
Organic dried fruits, honey, tahini, cashew
butter, almond butter, macadamia nut
butter, nuts, olives, olive oil, sun-dried
tomatoes, dried shiitake mushrooms, dulse,
and vanilla beans.
P. O. Box 10082
Berkeley, CA 94709
www.livingtreecommunity.com
jesse@livingtreecommunity.com
Phone: 800-260-9516; 510-526-7106

119

Maine Coast Sea Vegetables
Dulse, smoked dulse, digitata (kombu),
kelp, alaria, laver (wild nori),
sea seasonings: 1.5 oz. shakers of
dulse/garlic, kelp/cayenne, nori/ginger,
nori, dulse, kelp, sea chips, sea pickles, etc.
3 Georges Pond Road
Franklin, ME 04634
www.seaveg.com
Email: info@seaveg.com
Phone: 207-565-2907

Maine Seaweed Company
Dulse, alaria, kelp, laver (wild nori), digitata
kelp, bladderwrack, and Ascophyllum
Seaweed for gardeners to use as fertilizer.
PO Box 57
Steuben, ME 04680
www.maineseaweedcompany.com
Phone: 207-546-2875

New England Natural Bakers
Organic cereals, granolas, cereal bars, trail
mix bars, trail mixes
74 Fairview Street
East Greenfield, MA 01301
Phone: 413-772-2239
Fax: 413-772-2936

Now Foods
Organic grains, beans, flours, herbs, oils
and seeds
395 S. Glen Ellyn Road
Bloomingdale, IL 60108
www.nowfoods.com
Email: sales@nowfoods.com
Phone: 800-999-8069; 630-545-9098

Omega Nutrition USA Inc.
Organic oils
6515 Aldrich Road
Bellingham, WA 98226
www.omegaflo.com
Email: info@omegaflo.com
Phone: 360-384-1238; 800-661-3529

Organic Connection
Specializing in organic meat and poultry,
organic gourmet lines, including organic,

gluten-free breads and pasta, sheep and
goat dairy products.
PO Box 381
South Salem, NY 10590
www.organicconnection.net
Email: mail@organicconnection.net
Phone: 800-97-ORGANIC; 914-533-2170

Organic Valley Family of Farms
Milk, cheeses, eggs, poultry, meats, juice
CROPP Cooperative
507 West Main Street
LaFarge, WI 54639
www.organicvalley.com
organic@organicvalley.com
Phone: 888-444-6455

South River Miso Company
Organic mellow and aged misos: barley,
brown rice, sweet white rice, millet,
chickpea, aduki rice, black soybean barley,
dandelion leek, koji, and tamari.
888 Shelburne Falls Road
Conway, MA 01341
Phone: 413-369-4057

Spectrum Organic Products, Inc.
Maker of organic and natural products,
including Spectrum Essentials essential fatty
acid nutrition oils, and Spectrum Naturals
culinary oils, olive oils, vinegars,
mayonnaise, salad dressings and more.
1304 South Point Boulevard., Suite 280
Petaluma, CA 94954
www.spectrumorganic.com
Email: info@spectrumorganic.com
Phone: 800-995-2705
Fax: 707-765-8470

Timber Crest Farms
Organic and preservative-free dried fruits,
nuts, tomatoes and specialty foods. No
additives, no attitude.
4791 Dry Creek Road
Healdsburg, CA 95448
www.timbercrest.com
Email: tcf@timbercrest.com
Phone: 888-374-9325
Fax: 707-433-8255

Organic Information Resources

Acres USA
Publisher of *Acres* magazine; they also carry many helpful books, audio and video tapes on organic agriculture.
www.acresusa.com
Email: info@acresusa.com
Phone: 512-892-4400; 800-355-5313

Alliance for Sustainability
A fine organization based out of the University of Minnesota, supporting organic, sustainable agriculture.
www.iasa.org
Email: iasa@mtn.org
Phone: 612-331-1099; 800-260-2424

Global Safe Food Alliance
Organic and preservative-free dried fruits, nuts, tomatoes and specialty foods. No additives, no attitude.
www.purefood.org (see OCA)

Life Media/Natural Life Marketplace
Canadian source of complete natural living products; publisher of a magazine and supplier of books as well.
www.life.ca
Email: media@life.ca
Phone: 519-442-1404; 800-215-9574

Organic Consumer's Alliance (OCA)
Become involved in addressing key issues to insure the future of our food—and our health. Food safety, industrial agriculture, genetic engineering, irradiation, corporate accountability, globalization, mad cow disease and more. Free online newsletter.
www.organicconsumers.org
Email: loranda@organicconsumers.org
Phone: 218-226-4164

Organic Trade Association (OTA)
For information regarding organic standards and products. The OTA also sells an *Annual North American Organic Resource Directory*.
www.ota.com
Email: info@ota.com
Phone: 413-774-7511

Index

Alphabetical list of recipes

Index by Category

Shrimp Kabobs with Honey Mustard
  Sauce, 49
Thai Noodles with Chicken, Peppers
  and Caramelized Onion Sauce, 43

Salads

Arame Salad, 60
Baked Goat Cheese Salad, 55
Cucumber-Alaria Salad, 59
Five Element Salad, 58
Fruited Chicken Salad, 61
Pasta Salad with Goat Cheese, 54
Quinoa Tabouli Salad, 60
Salade Nicoise, 56
Smoked Salmon Salad, 54
Spinach and Shiitake Mushroom
  Salad with Creamy Herb Yogurt
  Dressing, 57
Warm Spinach and Orange Salad, 58

Side Dishes

Baked Yams with Maple Lime Glaze, 96
Black Beans with Ginger and Mustard
  Greens, 91
Chick Peas with Tomatoes and
  Ginger, 88
Curried Cauliflower, Potatoes and
  Chick Peas, 90
Dulse and Kale, 92
Gingered Tofu, 94
Italian Greens, 93
Italian Style Vegetable Stew, 99
Kale with Soy Garlic Butter, 91
Maple Cornbread, 88
Mediterranean Spinach, 93
Paradise Rice, 99
Pasta Italian Style, 97
Stuffed Artichokes, 89
Thai Peanut Stir Fry, 98
The Healthy Habit Veggie Burger, 95
Winter Vegetables, 95

Soups

Caribbean Ginger Carrot Soup, 85
Chilled Cucumber Soup, 84

Cream of Mushroom Soup, 82
Cream of Spring Greens Soup, 76
Creamy Spinach Tofu Soup, 78
Curried Vegetable Soup, 74
Energy Soup, 86
Granny's Chicken Soup, 83
Leek, Potato and Carrot Pottage (or
  "Soupe de Meme"), 75
Lentil Fresh Herb Soup, 81
Potato Leek Soup, 74
Roasted Yellow Pepper and Corn Milk
  Gazpacho, 77
Shiitake Tastebud Soup, 79
Sweet Fish Chowder, 83
Tomato Spinach Soup, 80
Winter Squash Kelp Soup, 79

Vegetarian Main Courses

Asparagus, Leek, Flax and Sunflower
  Tart, 30
Black-Eyed Peas with Spinach and
  Herbs, 24
Cheesey Eggy Casserole, 32
Creamy Mushroom Tempeh with Tofu
  Sour Cream, 35
Escarole and Beans, 31
Fabulous Lentil Stew, 29
Golden Quinoa with Yellow Peppers, 22
Herbed Goat Cheese-filled Pasta with
  Roasted Red Pepper Sauce, 26
Japanese Breaded Tofu with Red
  Pepper Lemon Sauce, 38
Marinated Baked Tofu, 36
Marinated Tempeh Kebobs, 28
Pasta Ratatouille with Purple Basil
  and Goat Cheese, 25
Red Chile, Mole Enchilada
  Casserole, 23
Roasted Corn and Pepper Chili, 39
Stir-Fry Brown Rice, Tofu and
  Veggies, 33
Sweet Potato and Bean Burritos, 34
Tempeh Sloppy Joe, 27
Thai Coconut Basil Sauce over Tofu
  and Vegetables, 37
Tofu Broccoli Quiche, 30
Vegetarian Chili, 39

OTHER TITLES FROM
VITAL HEALTH PUBLISHING:

Trace Your Genes to Health, Chris Reading, M.D., Ross Meillon, 336 pages, 1-890612-23-5, $15.95.

Smart Nutrients (2nd ed.), Abram Hoffer, M.D., Ph.D., Morton Walker, D.P.M., 224 pages, 1-890612-26-X, $14.95.

Our Children's Health: America's Kids in Nutritional Crisis, Bonnie Minsky, L.C.N., M.A., M.P.H., Lisa Holk, N.D., 296 pages, 1-890612-27-8, $15.95.

Healthy Living: A Holistic Guide to Cleansing, Revitalization and Nutrition, Susana Lombardi, 112 pages, 1-890612-30-8, $12.95.

Stevia Sweet Recipes: Sugar-Free – Naturally! (2nd ed.), Jeffrey Goettemoeller, 200 pages, 168 recipes, 1-890612-13-8, $13.95.

Stevia Rebaudiana: Nature's Sweet Secret (3rd ed.), David Richard, includes stevia growing information, 80 pages, 1-890612-15-4, $7.95.

Nutrition in a Nutshell: Build Health and Slow Down the Aging Process, Bonnie Minsky, L.C.N., M.A., M.P.H., 200 pages, 1-890612-17-0, $14.95.

Wheatgrass: Superfood for a New Millennium, Li Smith, 164 pages, 1-890612-10-3, $10.95.

Energy For Life: How to Overcome Chronic Fatigue, George Redmon, Ph.D., N.D., 248 pages, 1-890612-14-6, $15.95.

The Cancer Handbook: What's Really Working, edited by Lynne McTaggart, 192 pages, 1-890612-18-9, $12.95.

Taste Life! The Organic Choice, Ed. by David Richard and Dorie Byers, R.N., 208 pages, 1-890612-08-1, $12.95.

Lecithin and Health, Frank Orthoefer, Ph.D., 80 pages, 1-890612-03-0, $8.95.

Natural Beauty Basics: Create Your Own Cosmetics and Body Care Products, Dorie Byers, R.N., 204 pages, 1-890612-19-7, $14.95.

Anoint Yourself With Oil for Radiant Health, David Richard, 56 pages, 1-890612-01-4, $7.95.

My Whole Food ABC's, David Richard and Susan Cavaciuti, 32 pages, color illustrations, children's, 1-890612-07-3, $8.95.

Healing Herb Rapid Reference, Brent Davis, D.C., 152 pages, 1-890612-21-9, $12.95.

The Asthma Breakthrough: Breathe Freely – Naturally!, Henry Osiecki, B.S. Sc. (Hons.), Grad. Dip. Nutr. 192 pages, 1-890612-22-7, $13.95.

OTHER TITLES
FROM ENHANCEMENT BOOKS:

The Veneration of Life: Through the Disease to the Soul, John Diamond, M.D., 80 pages, 1-890995-14-2, $9.95.

The Way of the Pulse: Drumming With Spirit, John Diamond, M.D., 116 pages, 1-890995-02-9, $13.95.

The Healing Power of Blake: A Distillation, edited by John Diamond, M.D., 180 pages, 1-890995-03-7, $14.95.

The Healer: Heart and Hearth, John Diamond, M.D., 112 pages, 1-890995-22-3, $13.95.

Facets of a Diamond: Reflections of a Healer, John Diamond, M.D., approx. 324 pages, 1-55643-399-9, $16.95. (With North Atlantic Books)

Someone Hurt Me, Susan Cavaciuti, 48 pages, color illustrations, children's, 1-890995-20-7, $8.95.

I Love What I Do: A Drummer's Philosophy of Life at Eighty, Sam Ulano, 168 pages, 1-890995-35-5, $14.95.

Music and Song, Mother and Love, John Diamond, M.D., 132 pages, 1-890995-33-9, $13.95.

Holism and Beyond: The Essence of Holistic Medicine, John Diamond, M.D., 48 pages, 1-890995-37-1, $8.95.

On Wings of Spirit: The American Physician's Poetry Association Anthology, Ed. by John Graham-Pole, M.D., and Chuck Joy, M.D., 152 pages, 1-890995-32-0, $14.95.

VITAL HEALTH PUBLISHING
PO Box 152, Ridgefield, CT 06877
Website: www.vitalhealth.net
Inquiries: info@vitalhealth.net
Orders: 1-877-VIT-BOOK
Fax: 203-894-1866